# Praise for *The Fed-Up Man of Faith*

"Rabbi Shmuley has the courage to take on a subject that most simply accept as a way of life. *The Fed-Up Man of Faith* provides answers to questions that have plagued humans since they first experienced suffering. You will be hard-pressed to find a more thought-provoking book."
**Dr. Phil McGraw,** *host,* The Dr. Phil Show

"For years Rabbi Shmuley and I studied the Biblical texts relating to human reblliousness in the face of what some might believe is divinely ordained suffering. Standing up to God to protest the pain and death of innocents is a strong and inspiring pillar of Jewish wisdom and faith: wisdom that is so urgently needed now. Rabbi Shmuley has written a powerful, moving, and unprecedented book which gives eloquent voice to the critical spirit of human defiance."
**Rt. Hon. Cory Booker,** *Mayor of Newark*

"To the ancient questions of theodicy, Shmuley Boteach offers not a solution but Isaiah's cry: 'How Long, O Lord?' In this book, his first to record what has been for many years his most distinctive theological stance, Rabbi Shmuley insists that the only proper response to injustice is to challenge God for letting it occur. Provocative and heartfelt, the book offers a distinctive approach to the problems of suffering and evil."
**Noah Feldman,** *Bemis Professor of International Law, Harvard University*

"Rabbi Boteach is devout, but inquisitive. He combines reverence with sly jokes, humane reflection with provocation. He entertains, while focusing on serious matters. He is very much worth reading."
**Douglas J. Feith,** *Hudson Institute Senior Fellow; former Under Secretary of Defense*

"Shmuley Boteach...focuses on life's deepest questions and his thoughts are both surprising and sometimes provocative. Indeed he is one of the most truly imaginative thinkers in the Jewish world today. As you will see from his book, he often defies the establishment and crosses what many consider impenetrable barriers. This one is really worth reading."
**Michael Steinhardt,** *Wall Street legend; co-founder, Birthright Israel*

"In *The Fed-Up Man of Faith* Rabbi Shmuley tackles the greatest conundrum of all time. How can a loving God allow tragedy to occur in our lives? With great history and precision, the Rebbe not only tells us it is permissible to be angry at God when necessary, but also he explains how Judaism demands it. This is great comfort for those of us who are spiritual seekers, and who continually struggle to define our relationship with our creator."
**Alan Colmes,** The Alan Colmes Show; *author of* Thank the Liberals for Saving America

"There is a long tradition in Judaism of shaking one's fist at the sky and boldly challenging God. Drawing on Job, Rabbi Boteach has written an important book to guide questing and unsettled souls."

**Rabbi David Wolpe**, *Sinai Temple in Los Angeles; author of* Why Faith Matters

"Painful questions gnaw away at all people who take religious faith seriously, whether they are Jewish, Muslim, Christian or anything else. Now Rabbi Boteach provides us with clear answers and spiritual support. His ideas are like scaffolding around the rock of our faith: they not only help to hold it up but they enable us to climb higher and see further. This book is essential reading for those who think hard about their beliefs."

**Uri Geller**, *www.urigeller.com*

"As we face the curveballs, peaks and valleys of life's journey, it's reassuring to know that leaders such as Rabbi Shmuley Boteach are there to help us find meaning in the toughest of times."

**Josh Mandel**, *Treasurer of Ohio, two-tour Iraq War veteran, US Marine Corps*

"Shmuley reminds us how pertinent our struggle is; we can never accept the status quo whilst suffering remains. This provokes the question: can we eradicate suffering altogether? Must we? The answer flies right back at us in the form of another question: what are you doing to reduce another's suffering? Brilliant!"

**Kevin Bermeister**, *founder, Jerusalem 5800; founding investor, Skype*

"Rabbi Boteach formulates an understanding of the Jewish response to grief and loss that rings true, with readily digestible stories and proofs from biblical sources.... He makes the case for the only response to life's tribulations that is appropriate. This is a book that should be read by all who have suffered, or those who wish to gain a deeper understanding of life."

**Ronald Strobel, MD**, *cardiologist*

"Rabbi Shmuley is his irreverent self in this take-no-prisoners clarion call for moral accountability. This is straight talk about the big stuff. Read it. Love it. Then go out and make the world better!"

**Lisa Bloom**, *The Bloom Firm; author of the best seller* Think
*and the new book* Swagger

"Once again Rabbi Shmuley courageously challenges the status quo! His brilliant new book *The Fed-Up Man of Faith* is a must-read for anyone seeking to investigate our long-held notions about human suffering. Is it ever justified? Why do we so often glorify human suffering? Rabbi Shmuley invites us and urges us to go along with him and relentlessly question."

**Heidi Weisel**, *celebrated fashion designer*

# THE **FED-UP**
# MAN OF FAITH

# THE FED-UP
# MAN OF FAITH
Challenging God in the Face of Tragedy and Suffering

# SHMULEY BOTEACH

## Foreword by Dennis Prager

gefen
publishing house
JERUSALEM • NEW YORK
Est. 1981

Some of the material in this book previously appeared in essay form in the *Huffington
Post* and the *Jerusalem Post*. Permission to reprint is gratefully acknowledged.

Scriptural quotations are taken from THE HOLY BIBLE, NEW INTERNATIONAL
VERSION®, NIV® Copyright © 1973, 1978, 1984, 2011 by Biblica, Inc.™ Used by
permission. All rights reserved worldwide.

Cover Design: BIGraphics Creative Designers
Typesetting: Irit Nachum
Author photo: Shterna Boteach
ISBN: 978-965-229-606-1

1 3 5 7 9 8 6 4 2

Gefen Publishing House Ltd.
6 Hatzvi Street
Jerusalem 94386, Israel
972-2-538-0247
orders@gefenpublishing.com

Gefen Books
11 Edison Place
Springfield, NJ 07081
516-593-1234
orders@gefenpublishing.com

This World: The Values Network
PO Box 61
Englewood, NJ 07631
Follow Rabbi Shmuley on his website, www.shmuley.com
and on Twitter @RabbiShmuley
Tag discussions on this book #fedupfaith

**www.gefenpublishing.com**

Printed in Israel

Library of Congress Cataloging-in-Publication Data

Boteach, Shmuel.
The fed-up man of faith : challenging God in the face of tragedy and suffering /
Rabbi Shmuley Boteach ; foreword by Dennis Prager.
p. cm.
ISBN 978-965-229-606-1
1. Suffering—Religious aspects—Judaism. I. Title.
BM645.S9B68 2012
296.3'118—dc23
2012036371

*To*

## Kevin and Beverley Bermeister

Loving friends who were my daughter's matchmakers,
steadfast backers of my vision to spread Jewish knowledge
and values to the corners of the earth,
stalwart supporters of Jewish causes worldwide and
global philanthropists dedicated to eradicating human
suffering wherever it exists;

*& in memoriam*

**to my brother-in-law**

## Bernard Borchiyahu Wachtel

who passed away during the writing of this book
and whom I loved like a brother even after he and my
sister divorced. You have my eternal gratitude for the
loving warmth you always showed me and my family,
for the pride you took in the books I wrote and the
speeches I gave, and most importantly, for the eight
amazing children you raised, who are your greatest
legacy and your life's achievement.

You are deeply missed; your memory will be an
everlasting blessing.

# CONTENTS

# FOREWORD

## BY DENNIS PRAGER

Rabbi Shmuley Boteach has written many important books. This one may be his most courageous, because it touches a third rail in human and religious life: how to regard unjust suffering.

Shmuley, as he is widely and affectionately known, is an Orthodox rabbi ("ultra-Orthodox," in fact). Yet he wages war against a basic message of all religions – or at least of most of their clergy and theologians – including of his own faith, Judaism. "Religion," he writes, "made the terrible error of casting itself in the role of God's defender and of pain's protector, when its primary obligation should be as *man's* defender and pain's obliterator."

This "terrible error" is the acceptance of unjust suffering – whether man-made (evil) or natural (so-called "acts of God").

In this *cri de coeur*, Shmuley rails against unjust suffering in all its forms. If you have been maimed by a drunk driver, suffer relentless physical pain, lost a child, or are a Tutsi who has seen his family hacked to death by machete-wielding Hutus, a Jew who lost every loved one to Nazi monsters, a Chinese person who was used for grotesque medical experiments by the Japanese, or a victim of Communist totalitarianism – the list of mass evils is almost endless – you have not been blessed.

Rather, to Shmuley, unjust suffering is quite simply a curse. He therefore wants all of us to devote our lives to obliterating it.

And if that means railing against God as well as against man, so be it. It is not for no reason that the name of Shmuley's – and my – religious group is *Israel*, which literally means "struggle with God."

A Muslim woman once called my radio show and had but one question for me: "Why aren't you a Muslim?"

I told her that while there are a number of reasons – including, admittedly, my upbringing and my society – the most significant one is probably this: the name of my religious affiliation, *Israel*, means "struggle with God," while the meaning of the word for her religion, *Islam*, means "submission to God."

"I'd rather struggle with God than submit to God," I told her.

Her response was as meaningful as it was gracious: "I understand. Thank you."

This book will challenge many Christians – who for both Shmuley and me constitute, in America in particular, a blessing to all the inhabitants of the greatest Judeo-Christian country ever created.

Given that the essence of Christianity is Christ's suffering for humanity – a suffering that gives Christianity its purpose and meaning, since it alone has given humanity a chance at redemption – many Christians see their own suffering as Christ-like. Suffering is therefore inherently meaningful, even religiously uplifting.

Although more than a few religious Jews have embraced the suffering-is-always-meaningful view, Judaism doesn't see it that way. For Judaism, it is no *mitzvah* to suffer. Rather, the great *mitzvah* is to reduce suffering.

In speeches to both Jews and Christians, I have often presented the following hypothetical situation: Imagine two groups of Americans – Jews and Christians – invited to a luncheon at a hotel. Each group is served somewhat overripe melon. Which group, I ask the audience, do you suppose will complain more?

The question is a rhetorical one. Just about everyone knows that the Jews will complain more. But why? In large measure, because Jews don't accept suffering – even on the minuscule level of overripe melon – while Christians are more likely to accept it.

To be honest, on a daily basis, I prefer the Christians' attitude. Complainers drive me crazy. But the larger point is also significant. One reason Jews around the world were so active on behalf of persecuted Soviet Jews was the Jews' lack of acceptance of unjust suffering. At the same time, very few Christians engaged in activism on behalf of Soviet Christians, who were frequently even more persecuted than Soviet Jews. Virtually every synagogue in the Western world had a giant "Save Soviet Jewry" banner hanging in front of it; I never saw a church with a "Save Soviet Christians" banner. Persecuted Christians then – and today – are largely seen by fellow Christians as engaged in the holy vocation of suffering like Christ, for Christ.

To his credit, however, Shmuley has not written an ode to Jews. He is at least as annoyed with his own group as he is with others. And he knows as well as any of us how much America's Christians have done to alleviate suffering and fight injustice at home and abroad.

If you are suffering terribly and are tired of well-meaning people – secular as well as religious – telling you that in some way you have been blessed through your pain, this may be the book you have been waiting for.

Yes, we can and we should convert our suffering into something positive, if at all possible. But it isn't always possible. There just isn't anything redeeming, ennobling, or positive about your husband or wife drifting away to the prolonged living death of Alzheimer's disease.

Shmuley heeds the Bible's call to hate evil and to obliterate as much natural suffering as we can. Though a deeply religious man, he has written a heartfelt *j'accuse* directed at both God and man, on behalf of all the world's suffering men and women.

Shmuley has written *Kosher Sex, Kosher Adultery*, and *The Kosher Sutra*, but this is the book that should come with an NC-17 rating. It is for grown-ups only.

*Dennis Prager is a nationally syndicated talk host, author most recently of the* New York Times *bestseller* Still the Best Hope: Why the World Needs American Values to Triumph, *and founder of PragerUniversity.com.*

# PREFACE

This is a book of faith. It is a book written by a rabbi with a passionate and absolute belief in God. I'm telling you that now because you may find that what's written in these pages is very different from the faith your priest, rabbi, imam, or minister told you to have. That faith was probably about submission and subservience to the will of God. It was a faith that declared God to always be in the right and humans to be sinful and therefore in the wrong. You have most likely been told that you're not allowed to question God and that all things happen for a good reason, even if it's not disclosed to us humans.

It was this kind of faith that opened up religion to the modern accusations of creating people who are obedient and who revel in suffering, who create myths in order to make sense of all the death that surrounds us, and who teach people to find meaning in their pain.

Make no mistake, like you I love God with every fiber of my being. And I am writing this book because I'm fed up, not only with all the bad things that happen to good people but also with the fraudulent faith that so many of us have been encouraged to embrace. A faith that has made us weak rather than strong. A faith that is an opiate for suffering rather than a call to alleviate pain. A faith that tells us to love a God Who allows children to die rather than demanding from our Creator that He abide by the same principles and teachings He communicated through the prophet Moses, namely, to always "choose life."

This book demands that we stop being subservient men and women of religion and instead become defiant and rebellious people of faith. We must stop excusing tragedy and the God Who allows it, and rather fulfill His commandment to all humanity to never witness the suffering of another in silence.

I ask you to have an open mind as you read. The book is filled with proofs from the Bible and the sacred writings to make its case. There is no sacrilege here; you will, I believe firmly, emerge from these pages with a far greater commitment to, and love for, God even as you emerge as a faith-warrior who is prepared to spar with God over the vexing question of human suffering. In so doing, whatever your religion, you will become an "Israelite," a person prepared to wrestle and spar with your Creator, as you were meant to.

# Acknowledgments

Monica Klein helped tremendously in creating structure for, and expertly editing, this manuscript. Her insightful suggestions and painful (for an author) but brilliant cutting meant that this book came in at a much more reasonable size than the original of about a thousand pages which would have had you growing old and suffering while reading it.

My friend, student, and colleague Daniel Abraham is a great scholar and has a fascinating mind. If I needed an obscure source he dug around and always found it. Daniel reviewed the entire manuscript and constantly gave important suggestions for the book, which made it deeper and more wide-ranging.

This is the second book my dear friends Ilan Greenfield and Michael Fischberger of Gefen Publishing House and I are doing together, and they have brought to bear their characteristic alacrity, ethics, and attention to detail. When I told them how quickly I wanted the book out, they set their incredible team in motion. The final, beautiful product is in your hands right now (or being read on your tablet). Kezia Raffel Pride, among the best editors in the business, brought her expert pen to perfecting the manuscript, and Lynn Douek brought her phenomenal organizational skills to gathering all the pieces of the book together until it was tightly bound between two handsome covers.

My brilliant friend Dennis Prager read this book in manuscript form, and in the lengthy conversations we had about the book he made important suggestions for improving and deepening it. He gave generously of his time as well in writing the insightful foreword. I am grateful for his moral clarity, his incisive comments, and his belief in my work. Dennis has been a lifelong inspiration and mentor to me.

Professor Elie Wiesel, the great humanitarian and Holocaust survivor, has been a teacher, mentor, guide, and inspiration to me ever since I read his twentieth-century classic *Night*, and more importantly, ever since I hosted him at Oxford when I was a young man. Since then our relationship has deepened not only with my consuming everything the great man writes but through the moving conversations we have had amid the incredible generosity of time he has given me. Professor Wiesel, as the Jewish people's greatest living son, is an inspiration to my people and to humanity the world over. But it is his unique approach to human suffering – to defy the heavens and hold God accountable for human tragedy (and especially the Holocaust) – that has cast him as the global voice of a suffering humanity.

Rabbi Harold Kushner wrote the definitive modern populist book on suffering. He is a man of unique warmth, humility, and moral courage. Harold and I had three public debates on our respective responses to suffering in the UK in 1999 (at the University of Oxford, at Cambridge, and in London). We have stayed in touch and I remain a foremost admirer of a man who has been a great teacher to millions. I am grateful to Rabbi Kushner for all he has taught me and for inspiring deep thought on my part into the theological problem of suffering.

But one teacher towers above all others: the definitive mentor and moral and spiritual inspiration of my life, Rabbi Menachem Schneerson, the Lubavitcher Rebbe, of blessed memory, who, more than any other person, taught me to wrestle with God and demand the coming of a more perfect world in the messianic epoch. No other individual has had a more formative and permanent influence on how I see the relationship between God and man and the respective responsibilities of both. The Rebbe changed the Jewish and larger world through his emphasis on Jewish protest theology, advocating that humans have the right and indeed the obligation not just to perfect the world but to demand from God that He participate in its repair. Few other religious leaders in history have given man a greater voice in his relationship with God than the Rebbe, and few others have so deeply comprehended and advocated for the infinite value of every human life. For the rest of my days I will count my Rebbe as the principal engine behind my commitment to leading a life, however imperfect, of public involvement and service.

My parents, Yoav Botach and Eleanor Paul, taught me by example to always involve myself in alleviating human suffering and never to turn a blind eye to those in agony. This book is inspired by their commitment to reducing human pain and helping those in need. The same is true of my brothers and sisters, Sara, Bar Kochva, Chaim Moishe, Ateret, and my sister-in-law Iris. All run homes which, recalling that of our patriarch Abraham, are open to countless guests, and all are involved in charitable support and work. I have always been in awe of just what good and generous people my siblings are and, truth be told, I have also been jealous.

My children – Mushki and her husband Arik, Chana, Shterny, Mendy, Shaina, Rochel Leah, Yosef, Dovid Chaim, and Cheftziba – are my joy, delight, and gladness. Nothing has been more important to me than simply raising kind, loving, warm, open-minded, dedicated, and moral children. To the extent that my children have earned some, or even most, of those all-important qualities, they deserve the primary credit because of the hard work they have done on their characters. While I would of course love to see them be successful in a professional way in life, nothing makes me prouder than seeing them as good people dedicated to practicing compassion and alleviating human suffering.

Finally, my wife Debbie is the warmest person I know and makes all the difference in my struggle to always be optimistic. There are few battles more important. My wife has made me believe in good people because she is rarely given to any selfish considerations and she is largely free from the constraints of ego. She strives to confer dignity on all whom she meets and makes everyone feel important. When I fail to follow her example she gently rebukes me. Not only has she taken away so much of my own suffering, but she has shown me that she is most proud of me not when I publish a book or give a speech but when I help people in need and alleviate their pain. This book is inspired by her example of living a life dedicated to increasing the happiness and honoring the value of others. She has earned God's blessing and I know that whenever I put her first and cherish her infinitely I bring the God Who so loves her more deeply into my life.

This book is my own small, inadequate but passionately argued offering to all those who have suffered. May He Whom the Psalms proclaims is "the Healer of shattered hearts" cure you of your pain and mend your shattered soul. May suffering be abolished from the earth and may the long-promised messianic era dawn quickly in our day.

Rabbi Shmuley Boteach
September 2012
Englewood, NJ

# INTRODUCTION

One of the more mystifying events of the Bible involves God commanding Abraham to sacrifice his son Isaac. What was God thinking? After all, He was the One Who would later declare all human sacrifice (and especially child sacrifice) an abomination.

The most insightful commentary I've seen on this episode comes from my teacher and mentor, the Lubavitcher Rebbe, Rabbi Menachem Schneerson, who says the key to the story is to see Isaac not as an individual but as the Jewish religion. Who was Isaac? He was Judaism. He was the inheritor of Abraham's convictions. He was the person who would continue Abraham's belief system. Were Isaac to be slaughtered, everything Abraham had taught in terms of the rejection of paganism, the belief in one God, and more would be lost.

The test, therefore, was this: Would Abraham follow God's commandment to kill off his religion or would he put his religion before God's will? What really mattered to Abraham? God or Judaism? And if these facets of faith were put in conflict, which would Abraham choose?

The religious fanatic is the person who has ceased to serve God and has instead begun to worship a particular religion, making faith into an idol rather than the basis for a relationship with our Creator. It is in this light that we can understand how Islamic fundamentalists, and extremists of other religions, can be prepared to violate God's express commandment against murder in order to strike a blow for the glory not of their deity, but of Islam or their particular faith.

People who are in a relationship with God are humble and do their utmost to refrain from judging others. Their experience of God's compassion leads them to be merciful and loving. Their proximity to the Perfect Being reminds them of inherent human fallibility. But what happens when those who arrogantly worship religion successfully advance the cause that their religion is more important than life itself? How do the humble and devout hold steadfast to our faith when the pain and anguish of such zealots devastates all that we as a nation – and as human beings – hold dear? How do we continue to pray to the God of our forefathers when, at times of great and unwarranted suffering, God does not act as He did in the sparing of Isaac but rather appears to do nothing to intervene?

Is this not among the most asked and most unanswerable questions of our time – and of all time? How do we believe in God with full faith, how do we worship and serve Him with an open heart when, in our experience, God appears to willingly tolerate the suffering of His innocent creations the world over?

So many of us are searching for a reason why people suffer. We want to redeem tragedy by giving it meaning. Suffering ennobles the spirit, we say. It makes us more mature. It helps us focus on what's important in life. It makes us more sensitive to the pain of our fellow creatures. I would argue that suffering has no purpose, no redeeming qualities, and any attempts to infuse it with rich significance are deeply misguided. The more we explain suffering, the more sanctuary we grant it in our lives. The less we accept it, the more we combat it. *Suffering is not redemptive, it is not ennobling, it is not a blessing, and it teaches us nothing, absolutely nothing, that we could not have learned by gentler means.*

The appropriate response to death is always life. And the Jewish response to suffering is to demand that God put an end to it.

# PART I

# A WORLD OF SUFFERING

# CHAPTER 1

# ANOTHER DAY THAT WILL LIVE IN INFAMY

---

I believe in the sun even when it is not shining
and I believe in love even when no one is there,
but I believe in God even when He is silent.
I believe through any trial there is always a way.
*(Found on the wall of a cellar in the Cologne concentration camp)*

---

We recently marked the eleventh anniversary of that cloudless September 11 morning when 2,823 unsuspecting members of New York's work force were either doused in ninety thousand liters of jet fuel, then incinerated in fires that reached temperatures of a thousand degrees Celsius, or else crushed beneath thousands of tons of concrete and steel, in what we now call simply 9/11. Among the victims at the World Trade Center, the comparatively lucky ones were those able to choose how they would die by plunging over a thousand feet to the cracked sidewalks and rubble-strewn pavement below. Their fatal jumps were witnessed the world over on live television and by countless bystanders including nearby classrooms full of terrified children.

Not long after the towers were hit, reports began streaming in about an attack on the Pentagon in Washington, DC, and later the heroic crashing of Flight 93 in Pennsylvania in an effort by the

3

passengers to avert still greater catastrophe. The impact of these two subsequent tragedies was different than that wrought by the destruction of the twin monoliths looming in Lower Manhattan, but the billowing clouds of smoke, smell of burning flesh, and cries of devastating grief were very much the same.

As someone who lives in New Jersey in a town that is part of the Greater New York City area, as an American, and as a human being, I was horrified by the images that surrounded me. The murderers who perpetrated these atrocities were condemned and marginalized around the globe as cold-blooded killers. But in parts of the Islamic world, the executors of these crimes were lionized as martyrs.

During lunch with a Christian leader a month after the attacks, I decried the monstrous terror over salad and kosher chicken, employing words like *heartless, merciless,* and even *demonic.* My respected colleague reached across the table and took hold of my hands. "Rabbi," he said, "why don't you just say *evil.* You have to grow more comfortable with using that word: *evil.* These people were not heartless. They were not crazed. They were evil."

His words made me reflect. Why wasn't I using the word *evil*? In the countless interviews I (and a thousand other pundits) had done since the outrages of September 11, I had rarely described the terrorists as evil. After all, good and evil ring with religious connotations. *Webster's* defines a good person as "virtuous, right, commendable." An evil person is deemed "morally reprehensible, sinful, wicked." To describe someone as evil is to presuppose a religious system of right and wrong. Hence, secular people rarely use these terms. They might say "immoral" or "unethical." But never "evil."

However, I am a rabbi and I had been invited to discuss the unspeakable tragedies of September 11 from the perspective of my faith.

I gave the matter further thought. I soon realized that using religious terminology to describe the events of September 11 would mean dragging God into what happened. Wouldn't that make Him guilty as well? Didn't He stand by idly as two jets laden with innocent passengers were flown at half the speed of sound into packed office buildings? Wasn't God's silence also a glaring indictment?

Mind you, God was not alone as a spectator. Observers around the world watched as men and women jumped to their deaths in an effort to escape the raging inferno. The reports of bystanders watching falling bodies plummet to the ground reminded me of a story I heard when I visited the site of the Auschwitz death camp in Poland. My guide and close friend Professor Jonathan Webber told me that many who visit the death camp are actually attracted by what he referred to as "the pornography of evil." Consciously or unconsciously, it is often this curiosity about the unspeakable atrocities that occurred there that draws visitors to the site.

Similarly, we all sat watching CNN on 9/11 as the horrific yet somehow scintillating events unfolded before our very eyes. This is not meant to criticize those who looked on. Humans are largely helpless in such situations. We are not supermen. We could not have flown faster than a speeding bullet to snatch the jumpers in mid-air. *We could not have walked into the flames to save the many innocent victims. But God is invulnerable. Why didn't He do something?*

Some religious leaders argue that God cannot (or will not) intervene in earthly affairs because He does not wish to tamper with human free choice. But couldn't He have done something behind the scenes? Couldn't the airport security metal detectors have beeped and exposed the terrorists? Couldn't their phone conversations have been intercepted? Could not God have strengthened the steel girders of the towers so that those thousands of lives crushed beneath the building's debris would have been spared?

In fact He did work such behind-the-scenes miracles for some individuals; we've all heard stories about people who were delayed getting to work in the Twin Towers that day by unusual events, and so on. But God did not orchestrate events to stop the entire catastrophe and save all the people. If He'd done so in complete silence, would any of us have been the wiser? Would any of us have protested the subjugation of our free choice?

I began to suspect that my subconscious refusal to use the word *evil* was somehow calculated to exonerate God – to place the guilt firmly on the shoulders of the perpetrators, making them wholly responsible for the murders. I was reluctant to use religious language that would raise the profound spiritual questions about why God allows evil to flourish and why the world He built does not always seem to reward goodness. Indeed, the good, rather than the wicked, are often the ones who seem to suffer most. In philosophy this is called "theodicy," reconciling the good God with the existential problem of suffering. But after my friend gently chided me for avoiding labeling this heinous act for what it was, I began to suspect I was part of a cover-up. By refusing to talk about the massacre within the framework of good and evil, was I colluding in a worldwide conspiracy to let God off the hook for the horrors of 9/11?

Launching a religious attack against the United States, the terrorists believed they were striking a blow for their deity and would earn the blessings of eternity for doing so. The "infidels" they chose to murder were also citizens of a God-revering nation, where 92 percent believe in the Almighty. I was reminded of the words of Abraham Lincoln during his second inaugural address, in his discussion of the war between North and South: "Both read the same Bible and pray to the same God, and each invokes His aid against the other.... The prayers of both could not be answered."[1] Fair enough. But why then were the prayers of one – the terrorists, who screamed "*Allahu akbar*" as they blasphemed by killing in the name of God – the prayers that were answered?

We humans will never know the reason an omnipotent God allowed a tragedy of this magnitude to take place. But by accepting our ignorance and God's inscrutability, do we, His faithful, let God escape scot-free? In commemorating the innocence and heroism of those who lost their lives that fateful day, do we in essence engage in the practice of a submissive, excuse-oriented faith, where man is always culpable and God is always beyond reproach and beyond reach?

Would those who fault America, as some religious leaders did in the aftermath of 9/11, have us embrace a fraudulent relationship with God? One where mankind is constantly found blameworthy and God is at all times innocent? I, myself, prefer the faith of Abraham, who pleaded with God for the lives of even the wicked inhabitants of Sodom and Gomorrah. I would opt to emulate the conviction of Moses, who told God if He punished the Israelites for the golden calf He must also remove the name Moses from the Bible, thereby severing their relationship and altering the future of the Jewish people forever.

Wouldn't you?

---

1  Cited in Peter B. Levy, *100 Key Documents in American Democracy* (Westport, CT: Praeger, 1999), 168.

# CHAPTER 2

# WHAT OF THE HOLOCAUST?

---

You shall not bow down to them or worship them; for I, the Lord your God, am a jealous God, punishing the children for the sin of the parents to the third and fourth generation of those who hate me... *(Exodus 20:5)*

---

Fifty-five years ago at the Nuremberg trials, Yosef Mengele, the infamous "doctor" of Auschwitz, was accused in absentia of "throwing live children into bonfires; conducting medical experiments on living prisoners, especially twins, by injecting their eyes, spines and brains with camphor and other chemicals; shooting children in order to perform autopsies on them; exposing healthy prisoners to yellow fever and extreme X-ray radiation for study; sterilizing and castrating prisoners; and cutting off body parts of female prisoners for use in performing tissue cultures."[1]

There are theologians who maintain the Holocaust was divine punishment upon the sinful – with some Jewish leaders saying it originated in Germany because the Jews there were assimilating en masse.

---

1  *New York Times*, cited in David Birnbaum, *God and Evil: A Unified Theodicy/ Theology/Philosophy* (Hoboken, NJ: Ktav, 1989), vii.

In front of a large crowd I debated a leading Jewish-Christian missionary who maintained that the Holocaust, like so many other calamities in Jewish history, was a punishment measured out by God for Jews' rejection of Jesus.

But could anybody possibly have been so sinful as to warrant the horror of Auschwitz? Or a better question: Could *everybody* have been so sinful? Is there any sin so heinous that it could demand that one and a half million children be gassed to death? Is Jesus, who called himself the prince of peace, so vengeful as to call upon God to allow the torture and murder of millions of Jews simply because they went to synagogue rather than to church?

Even if we embrace the Eastern concept of karma, and accept that the victims of the Holocaust were recycled souls, is there anything that any one of them could have done in a previous life to have earned such unspeakable cruelties? If these theologians are right and the Holocaust was some sort of divine retribution for the sins of man, who would want to be associated with a god that metes out such punishment? Who could possibly *love* such a god? And who among us would wish to worship him?

When my daughter Shterny was sixteen years old, she chose to study three great novels of Nobel Peace Prize laureate Elie Wiesel for a school project. When the assignment was completed, Professor Wiesel, a hero of mine whom I had hosted twice as a lecturer at Oxford and multiple times in New York and even Utah, kindly agreed to meet with my daughter to discuss her conclusions. My daughter, clearly intimidated by the presence of the great man, said in her tremulous little voice, "You were raised a very religious Jewish boy. Yet, you gave up your religion after watching so many of your family members and friends get killed by the Nazis. But later, you came back to it, you came back to God. Did you find that hard?"

Wiesel looked at her pensively. Then, in a quiet voice barely surpassing a whisper, he said, "The hard part was not reconnecting to God. The hard part was leaving Him in the first place. I grew up with God. He was my companion and my friend. But then He abandoned us. I never questioned His existence, only His goodness. But I missed Him so much that I had to come back. Our relationship is very different right now. It's more honest, but it is also more sad."

In 2003, I visited Berlin as a speaker at the Ecumenical Church Day, which draws some two hundred thousand of Germany's young people. At that time the German Holocaust Memorial, located in central Berlin just a block from the Reichstag, was under construction. I was eager to see how the German government had chosen to commemorate the Holocaust, but I had to wait till 2011, when I was invited to lecture to the Jewish communities of Cologne, Frankfurt, and Berlin, to see the project in its completion. Upon my arrival in the German capital I headed directly to the monument and museum with my son Mendy, at the time a rabbinical student in yeshivah in Frankfurt.

The memorial is a stunning and sobering site, consisting of thousands of coffin-like objects that form a maze. Underneath it is a small and powerful exhibit that concisely captures the horror of the crimes within the limitations of what a rendering can convey. Reading the panels and seeing the pictures of my people being slaughtered en masse brought great sadness but also rage – conflicting emotions made all the more unmanageable by the fact that I was feeling anger at the very people who constructed the memorial in acknowledgment of their responsibility for these atrocities.

One picture in particular left me numb. It was that of a little girl, about five years of age, who had just stepped off the train in Auschwitz. It was bitterly cold around her and she had no shoes. Yet she was playing with something in her hands, oblivious to the horror that surrounded her. No doubt she was dead less than an hour after the picture was taken, her young lungs filled with German poison gas.

I had a baby daughter at that time, who also toyed constantly with little objects in her hands and often ran around barefoot. My baby daughter always made my heart melt; my book *Honoring the Child Spirit* is dedicated to her. A father's compassion erupted in me in response to this little Jewish girl in the photograph who was so reminiscent of my own child. I was swallowed up by the magnitude of her parents' grief, unable to protect her little feet from the frost, unable to fill her tiny stomach with any kind of food, unable to protect her from the monsters that would devour her in so short a time.

At seven in the evening, a young German curator came to tell me and my son the museum would soon be closing. She did so very gently, almost sensing what I was feeling. She tried to engage us in conversation. We responded as warmly as we could. I felt her pain as well. She was saying, *I'm not one of them. I feel deeply for what happened to your people.* Emerging from the exhibit, we asked a passing German youth to take a picture of us, before realizing he was half drunk. He took the photo and then, through his insobriety, he also attempted to reassure us that he wasn't one of *them*. "It bothers me," he told us, "that many of the new Muslim immigrants here in Germany say Jews have stolen their land. It's wrong. The Jews have suffered enough. Why don't people leave them alone?" We thanked him for his sentiments as he staggered on.

At that very moment I understood that the German and Jewish peoples were forever locked in what Martin Luther King Jr. called a "single garment of destiny." Today's Germans feel self-conscious, linked to the Holocaust by the enormous guilt they still feel for the atrocities perpetrated by their parents and grandparents. Jews likewise feel self-conscious when confronted by today's Germans.

We are forced to engage our own conflicting emotions – rage at the destruction of the European Jewish legacy and extermination of our people, and remorse for implicating, even ever so slightly, a generation of Germans who, for the most part, want nothing more than to make amends.

In a larger sense, our two peoples are connected by something even more powerful and more vexing: the insoluble questions that tug at our basic humanity. For the Germans, the question is *How could we have done this? How could we have hated so deeply as to have become so unquenchably bloodthirsty? Are we humans or beasts?* For the Jews the question is very different, but equally unanswerable: **How could God have allowed this?** *Where was He when six million of His people were collected and massacred in sprawling concentration camps? And how could His creatures have chosen to commit such unprecedented crimes?*

# CHAPTER 3

# THERE ARE NO SMALL TRAGEDIES

---

I will set my face against you so that you will be defeated by your enemies; those who hate you will rule over you, and you will flee even when no one is pursuing you. *(Leviticus 26:17)*

---

From the unprecedented devastation of the Holocaust to the genocides in Cambodia and Kosovo, Rwanda, and Sudan, we have borne witness to men daily raping and murdering women and children with impunity, and to the massacre of the unprotected in the hundreds of thousands in the paradoxical name of ethnic cleansing.

In August 2012, in the middle of my campaign for the United States Congress, I traveled to Rwanda to highlight the importance of anti-genocide legislation as a central plank in my foreign policy platform. It was an emotionally devastating trip. Walking into the Ntarama Church outside Kigali and witnessing the scenes of mass slaughter all around, I instantly began to gag and ran outside lest I be sick in consecrated ground. I walked in several more times but could barely breathe. Never in my life had I seen something so utterly gruesome.

Eighteen years earlier, in April 1994, approximately five thousand Tutsi men, women, and children had sought refuge in the church to protect themselves from genocidal Hutu militiamen. But God sometimes hides and does not protect. After throwing grenades into the church, the Hutu monsters axed, macheted, clubbed, and speared every last person to death. Today, their skulls, bones, coffins, and blood-soaked clothing decorate the church in a macabre orgy of death that left me dizzy and weak. I considered myself fortunate not to have gone to another church, two hours away, where nearly five hundred lime-preserved bodies, in their crouching postures of death, lie strewn around the church after being found nearby in a mass grave. They remain there, unburied, silent witnesses to man's brutality to his fellow man.

The night before I had sat with Marie-Jean, a Tutsi woman in her forties whose husband was hacked to death in front of her eyes when Hutu militiamen broke into their home. They ripped her eight-month-old baby from her arms and dashed her brains against a wall. Then it was her turn, as she was savagely gang-raped by more than ten HIV-positive men, leaving her with AIDS. She is an attractive and bright-eyed woman. I asked her if she would ever marry again. She answered that she would never allow any man to ever touch her again. She added that she stays alive only for her twenty-year-old son, who miraculously survived.

In Rwanda the scars of death are much fresher than in the German death camps of Poland. The survivors of the fastest genocide in human history are not octogenarians from my Jewish community but vibrant twenty- and thirty-somethings. Each has soul-searing stories of entire families being dismembered by machetes, often by their own neighbors and family friends. The stories do not come naturally. Rwandans have not learned to talk easily about the horrors they experienced. Their stories come out only when they have learned to trust you. One guide drove us around for two days. As he left us at our hotel in Kigali, he suddenly said, "My grandparents, father, mother, brother, and sister were all killed. I was fourteen. I survived living in broken-down homes that the Hutus were not searching." A few minutes later, he drove off.

Lieutenant General Charles Kayonga, commander-in-chief of the Rwandan army, whom I met through my daughter who is serving in the Israeli army and who is part of a unit that hosted him in Israel, witnessed the entire genocide as a young RPF officer stationed in Kigali. A soft-spoken man of probing intelligence and a deep listener, he is a hero who commanded a battalion that was surrounded by tens of thousands of Hutu killers yet still saved as many lives as he could. He told me that, given their experience, the Rwandans often see themselves as the Jews of Africa. Like the Jews of the Holocaust, the Tutsis found themselves alone; few nations cared that they were being slaughtered.

The United States and the United Nations were especially indifferent. President Clinton did not have even a single meeting with his senior staff throughout the three months of the genocide and refused to even destroy or block the RTLM radio antenna through which the genocide was broadcast. Kofi Annan forbade UN peacekeeping chief General Romeo Dallaire from taking any action that would prevent the genocide. Dallaire pleaded but Annan was resolute and ordered the bulk of UN peacekeepers out of the country. I discovered that the Rwandans are, like Israel, highly suspicious of the UN and especially of the French, whom, they argue, aided and abetted the genocide by training Hutu militiamen. Rwandan enmity toward the French continues till today.

I met several Rwandan youth who had never left the country but told me if they did, the first country they would visit would be Israel, which seems to be something of a role model to Rwandans steeped in their recent history. I found it inspiring that they connected so deeply with my people, but also sad that a principal component of that connection was that both our people had experienced genocide.

But so often death of genocidal proportions happens through more natural means.

In the last few years, earthquakes leveled the already impoverished nation of Haiti and brought Japan again face-to-face with nuclear disaster. For these reasons and more, who among us has not struggled to emerge with our faith in an all-powerful God intact?

I visited Haiti with my eldest daughter three weeks after the earthquake to distribute supplies to orphanages. We drove through Port-au-Prince and had to cover our faces from the rotten stench of decaying human flesh that was everywhere in the air. I struggled just to breathe.

Perhaps the only preparation I had for the devastation of Haiti was having seen grainy black-and-white photographs of Berlin and Tokyo in the summer of 1945, cities reduced to endless stretches of rubble. Port-au-Prince looked like it had been bombed mercilessly from the air by a powerful foe.

It confronted us slowly. As we made the long drive from Santa Domingo and across the border into Haiti, we first thought to ourselves, *Thank goodness – the earthquake wasn't nearly as bad as described.* We saw a few homes that had collapsed on the outskirts of the city and heard the tragic story of a grandmother who had been crushed under a collapsed roof. But three hundred thousand dead? The estimates had to be exaggerated.

Then we got nearer and the tent and squatter cities of the endless number of homeless, sitting outside their makeshift abodes with little to do and a haunted appearance, began to hit us.

But only when we got into the very heart of the city – ground zero of the quake's devastation – did a world of pure destruction open before us. One out of every two buildings had collapsed like pancakes, creating giant tombs in the city's heart. The inescapable stench of death assailed us from every side. No one will ever know how many people were buried inside those mountains of wreckage. It took the ancient Roman Empire hundreds of years to collapse and become a city of ruins. But mother nature accomplished the task in Haiti in a matter of seconds.

As we drove through downtown, the scene was made even more macabre by the hundreds of people walking through the rubble like ghosts, seemingly barely cognizant of the apocalypse that was all around them. Barely a store was open. The electricity was long gone. But they walked through, determined, as if the heart of the city still beat.

The stench of death was all over my clothes. I picked it up while reviewing a collapsed nursing college that trapped about 180 young women. Their crushed skulls, feet, and hands – a deep blue color from rigor mortis – stuck out from the rubble. Some of their bodies had been eaten by stray dogs and the area was littered with vertebrae. We struggled not to step on the remains that were all around us. After that I was taken to see the hospital's morgue. Hundreds of bodies, so many children, looked like they were merely asleep.

Port-au-Prince was a pile of rubble. I thought to myself that it might take decades to clean it up.

I left Haiti feeling overwhelming grief for the devastation experienced by its inhabitants, a profound respect for their courage and how little they complain, and in awe of the human capacity to draw together to help those in need.

Shortly after my heart-wrenching visit to Haiti I traveled to Venice, Italy, to address the local Jewish community under the auspices of the Chabad rabbi, who is a friend. I addressed the issue of why a good God allows the innocent to suffer. I was amazed when an observant Jew approached me to say that the people of Haiti were not innocent, immersed as they are in voodoo, witchcraft, and idol worship. "Surely you don't mean to say that the morgue filled with the babies that I witnessed – the stench so bad that I was gagging – deserved to die? Or that the discarded bodies I saw at a collapsed nursing college, with vertebrae being eaten by scavenger dogs, deserved their fate?" His response: the people of Haiti as a whole were punished. A similar sentiment had earlier been voiced by my friend the Reverend Pat Robertson on *The 700 Club.*

I have always been puzzled as to why many religious people are prone to portraying God as chief executioner and are always finding reasons to justify human suffering. When Abraham is informed by God of His intention to annihilate Sodom and Gomorrah, he protests human suffering and challenges God. Raising his hands to the heavens, he exclaims, "Will not the Judge of all the earth do right?" (Genesis 18:25).

When God informs Moses that He will exterminate the Jews after the sin of the golden calf, Moses tells God, "then blot me out of the book you have written [the Torah, i.e., the Bible]" (Exodus 32:32). *I will risk severing my relationship with a God Who seemingly practices cruelty.* Yet, when New Orleans was nearly wiped off the map by Katrina, many religious people said it was punishment for the sexual immorality of Bourbon Street.

The Holocaust produced two camps of Jews. Many decided that the Jews had been punished for intermarriage and for wanting to be secular. But others had a more authentically Jewish response. They rejected any theological justification or self-blame and set to work even harder, some toward the regeneration of the Jewish people through immersion in Jewish study, and some toward the creation of a Jewish state where Jews would find refuge and build an army to prevent another genocide.

So many people search for a reason why people suffer. They want to redeem tragedy by giving it meaning. Suffering ennobles the spirit, they say. It makes you more mature. It helps you focus on what's important in life.

*I would argue that suffering has no purpose, no redeeming qualities, and any attempts to infuse it with rich significance are deeply misguided.*

Of course suffering can lead ultimately to a positive outcome. The rich man who had contempt for the poor and suddenly loses his money can become more empathic when he himself struggles. The arrogant executive who treats her subordinates like dirt can soften when she is told that she, God forbid, has breast cancer. But does it have to come about this way? Is suffering the only way to learn goodness? Is there not a painless way by which human nature is ennobled?

I saw how suffering can ennoble character in the moving conversation I had with the mother of Trayvon Martin, the African-American teenager who was fatally shot by a neighborhood watchman on February 26, 2012, as he was walking in a gated community in Sanford, Florida. The tragic story gripped America with sadness, outrage, and the senselessness of his loss. My dear friend Kathryn Milofsky arranged for me to speak with Trayvon Martin's mother, Sybrina Fulton, and her attorney Benjamin Crump, just before Passover. We had invited Trayvon's parents to our Passover seder, but as that could not be worked out I was grateful to speak to Ms. Fulton and offer her whatever words of comfort and healing I could muster.

The opposite turned out to be the case. It was I who found the conversation healing and inspirational and decided therefore, after asking her permission, to share it in a column on the holiday weekend holy to both Christians and Jews.

Ms. Fulton thanked me for the column I wrote about her son in the *Huffington Post*.[1] After expressing my heartfelt condolences on the tragic loss of her child, I asked her if she felt disappointed that some segments of our society may not understand the depth of her anguish.

She said that the key to understanding how she and her family felt was human empathy. Anyone who is a parent could appreciate what it might mean to lose a child, especially one who died under such appalling circumstances. To compound the pain, the feeling that there is no justice magnified the grief beyond measure. She said that this was not an issue for the black or white communities or the political right or left. It was a human issue, an issue for all parents, an issue that concerns anyone who appreciates life and opposes senseless tragedy.

"I look at my older son, who is twenty-one years old. And I see Trayvon in him. And I keep on expecting Trayvon to come home. But he doesn't come home. And now, I have one son on earth, and one son in heaven. And I miss him."

I asked her if she felt any anger toward George Zimmerman, who fired the shot that killed Trayvon.

"I have no time for anger. I don't want to grant it a place in my heart. I simply want justice. I don't hate him and I'm not angry at him. But my son died and we deserve to know what happened. It's not for the police to determine justice. It's for the courts. And we'll stand by what the court says. But that's what I'm focused on. We want an arrest. But it's not out of anger or hatred. I have too much to do to be sidetracked with any of that. But when your son dies and there isn't even an arrest, it makes it so much harder."

---

1   "Trayvon Martin and Race: A Sober Assessment," March 30, 2012.

She uttered these words in a pained tone. She did not raise her voice. There was no malice or rancor. She spoke passionately and with deep conviction.

I asked her if she felt anger at God over her son's tragic death. She immediately quoted Proverbs 3:5, citing both chapter and verse: "Trust in the Lord with all your heart and lean not on your own understanding."

She said she was finding comfort in the verse. She does not question God. She was asking for understanding. "At first, I kept on asking why me, why Trayvon. But now I know that God has called Trayvon. He was chosen. His name is now known throughout the country and throughout the world. He is a symbol of the fight against injustice. People understand that there has to be fairness and righteousness. And they're learning it from Trayvon."

I told her that I was amazed that she had quoted that verse. The first Hebrew word in the verse is *betach* – trust. It's my name, Boteach. And because my family name translates literally as Trust, I had chosen that verse as my main verse for my junior high school yearbook, and had adopted it as a mantra by which I have attempted to lead my life.

I asked her if she believed in America as a place of fairness and justice. She said she did. "But that's why this case is so important. If Trayvon can die and no one pays a price, it can be someone else's child next time. This isn't only about our family, it's about all families. It's about all children. Trayvon is everyone's child."

As she spoke I was reminded of Martin Luther King's famous words, "Injustice anywhere is a threat to justice everywhere."[2]

I asked her how her family was coping. She said the tragedy had drawn the entire family closer. They were sharing many

---

2   "Letter from Birmingham Jail," April 16, 1963.

family meals, they were comforting each other, finding solace in one another.

I found her words, her voice, her demeanor, her compassion, and her conviction uplifting. Here was a mother who had buried her son under the most tragic circumstances. Yet she spoke without rage, hatred, or spite. She spoke of feeling God's presence in her heart and in her life. She said that other parents had to understand her campaign. That if anything like this had happened to their children, they too would shake heaven and earth to demand justice.

Before ending the conversation, I told her that the black and Jewish communities are united not by a shared history of pain or suffering, but a shared history of spiritual promise and social redemption. That through all our trials and tribulations our two communities had always turned to God as the rock of our salvation, finding solace in His loving embrace. She echoed the sentiment and spoke of the all-encompassing presence of God in her life.

We agreed that we would, God willing, meet up when she was in New York. As I ended the conversation I felt as though I had been speaking with a giant, a woman of extraordinary heart, though it be shattered into a million pieces.

And I have met many such incredible people whose hearts were enlarged through suffering.

Indeed, I have found myself many times becoming more sensitive, caring, and empathetic when I have been put through very difficult ordeals, involving fear and uncertainty. When I have been afraid of something terrible happening, God forbid, I have found myself so much more open to the pain and suffering of others. I have found I become more humble, less judgmental, and more approachable. But notwithstanding this truth, I know that I have no excuse not to be this way even when I don't suffer. By becoming more loving when I am in pain I am lending darkness a blessedness that it does not deserve. Love should come through light, and understanding should come through joy. Yes, they can come through gloom and pain. But why lend anguish a dignity it has not earned and should not receive?

I am adamant that these people who show so much courage through suffering are special not *because* of what they suffered but *despite* what they suffered. Trayvon's mother is not unique because her son died but because she brought him into this world with love and her love continues past the grave. It is not how she bears his death that makes her special but how she continues to hold on to his life.

Jewish values maintain that there is no good that comes from suffering that could not have come through a more blessed means. Some people win the lottery and are so humbled that they dedicate a huge portion to charity. Yes, Tiger Woods confessed to the corruption that came through his celebrity. He betrayed his marriage on numerous occasions and paid for it by losing his family. But a rock star like Bono becomes rich and famous and consecrates it to the relief of poverty. The Holocaust led directly to the creation of the State of Israel, I agree. But there are plenty of nations that came into existence without a losing a third of their number in gas chambers.

Here is another way that Jewish values are strongly distinguished from other value systems. Many religions believe that suffering is redemptive. In Christianity, the suffering servant, the crucified Christ, brings atonement for the sins of mankind through his own torture. The message: no suffering, no redemption. Someone has to die so that the sins of mankind are erased. Suffering is therefore extolled in the New Testament: "Not only so, but we also glory in our sufferings, because we know that suffering produces perseverance; perseverance, character; and character, hope" (Romans 5:3–4). Again, "If we are distressed, it is for your comfort and salvation; if we are comforted, it is for your comfort, which produces in you patient endurance of the same sufferings we suffer" (2 Corinthians 1:6). Indeed, Paul even made suffering an obligation, encouraging the fledging Christians to "share in suffering like a good soldier of Christ Jesus" (2 Timothy 2:3).

But Judaism, in prophesying a perfect messianic future where there is no death or pain, ultimately rejects the suffering-is-redemptive narrative. Suffering isn't a blessing, it's a curse. Jews are obligated to alleviate all human misery. Suffering leaves you bitter rather than blessed, scarred rather than humble. Few endure suffering without serious and lasting trauma. Suffering leads to a tortured spirit and a pessimistic outlook. It scars our psyches and creates a cynical consciousness, devoid and bereft of hope. It makes us envious of other people's happiness. If individuals do become better people as a result of their suffering, it is a result of personal strength: ennoblement of character comes through triumph over suffering rather than its endurance.

Speak to Holocaust survivors like Elie Wiesel and ask them what they gathered from their suffering, aside from loneliness, heartbreak, and a sense of outrage. To be sure, they also learned the value of life and the sublime quality of human companionship. Wiesel is an incredibly profound man. But couldn't these lessons, this depth, have been learned through life-affirming experiences that do not leave all of one's relatives as ash?

There can be no doubt – as so many who have suffered tell me – that suffering can lead to deep insights about life. It can make us more sensitive. People who have divorced and then remarried have told me that their second marriages are often much more insightful. They can also give better advice to colleagues and offer a compassionate listening ear to others, having been through the pain and agony of divorce. Parents who have lost children have told me that they are able to comfort other bereaved parents far more deeply because of their experiences, because of their broken and shattered hearts. Those who have been through war-torn areas have told me how much more they appreciate life and the freedoms and liberties they gain upon coming to the West. I do not deny that any of this is true.

*Of course we say that suffering can be a great teacher, but I believe that the pain and scar tissue is absolutely not worth the price. I also believe that the great lessons that suffering can teach us can be learned without suffering.* For example, would those couples who think their marriages have been enriched through the pain of a prior divorce really not be able to have deep and fulfilling conversations without having suffered? Is it really not possible for us to enjoy the blessings of freedom and liberty even if we haven't been deprived of them? Can life itself not be a teacher? Can we only appreciate the beauty and wonders of our children once they are taken from us, God forbid? Is it not possible to see beauty and wonder in their childlike drawings and the cute questions they ask us, in their innocent eyes and their warm hands slipped into ours?

No, I reject suffering and will not dignify it as a teacher.

I have met people who have been softened by suffering. But I have also met people possessed of the most charitable hearts who give simply because they know they are blessed and they feel obligated to share their blessings with others. There are poets and scientists whose creativity derives directly from their tortured spirits. Michelangelo, arguably the greatest artist of all time, scribbled, in the margin of one of his notebooks, a large hand with human figures, accompanied by expressions of aching pain and regret such as "Death is the end of a dark prison" and "Desire engenders desire and then leaves pain." Sylvia Plath suffered from deep depression throughout her life and when her husband, the poet Ted Hughes, left her for another woman, she committed suicide at the tender age of thirty, orphaning her two children. There can be no question that Michael Jackson's beautiful lyrics about his soul's longing for the innocence of childhood stemmed from the adversity of his early years and the lifelong emptiness he felt for his fame. He details the depth of this pain and anguish in the thirty hours we recorded together for publication in the book *The Michael Jackson Tapes*.

But for every one of these artists who draw some sort of inspiration from torment we can find a William Shakespeare, whose life and career does not indicate creativity born of inner torture or turmoil, and an Albert Einstein, who was raised by two loving parents in a stable environment and enjoyed a childhood without major traumatic incident.

My parents' divorce drove me to a deeper understanding of life and a greater embrace of religion. Yet, I know people who have led completely privileged lives and have far deeper philosophies of life and are more devoted to their religion than I am. And they have the advantage of not being bitter, cynical, or pessimistic the way I can sometimes be because of the pain of my early childhood.

As rabbi at Oxford University I noticed that the college students I knew who were raised in homes in which their parents gave them huge amounts of love and attention were the most healthy and balanced of all. They were usually also the best students. Those who were demeaned by their parents could also be positive and loving, but a Herculean effort was first needed to undo the scarring inflicted upon them by parental neglect. Whatever good we receive from suffering can be brought about in a painless, joyful manner. And it behooves people of faith, especially, to cease justifying the death of innocents once and for all and instead to rush to comfort and aid the survivors.

But one need not look only at grand-scale catastrophes to be plagued by cosmic questions. The death of even one innocent victim is enough to crush our belief in a benevolent Creator. In July 2011 the nation heard all the tragic details that led up to the horrific murder of Leiby Kletzky – an eight-year-old Orthodox Jewish boy, walking home from day camp for the very first time all by himself. Forever seared in my memory are the surveillance videos showing Leiby coming to each street corner searching for the correct path to his house. From street to street he wanders, wondering whether this is the place he's supposed to turn to make his way back home.

I couldn't help but wonder, is this not the human story? Hopeful and earnest, trying to find our way forward in our lives? Going from crossroad to crossroad, attempting to make the right turn, as we long for the place we call home? We, too, can lose our way, given the complexities of modern-day lives. We also turn to others for help and guidance, often learning the hard way the consequences of misplaced trust.

In Leiby's awful case, he comes across a monster named Levi Aron, who subsequently murders him and commits one of the more grotesque acts anyone can imagine.

This was an event that beggared belief. In most cases where, say, a pedophile abducts and murders a child, he has made that child a mark well before the incident. He has gone to playgrounds to hone in on a child as a target and slowly lures that child to his lair. But Leiby, with the open unblemished heart of any child, ends up asking the one fiend (or so we hope) that lives in the neighborhood to help him find his way. Could God not have had the child simply remember the street corner where he was supposed to turn? Could He not have supplied a familiar marker? And even if the child was lost, could God, with an invisible outstretched arm, not have steered Leiby toward one of the thousands of people who would have happily returned him to his parents?

One reason observant Jews live together is to protect their children from corrosive influences, to filter out elements of the popular culture and media unhealthy to a child's development. They take comfort in raising their families in a community surrounded by people who are never truly strangers. Their neighbors share their faith, their values, their way of life. No one's kids are ever in danger, and if one family is in trouble all the rest come to the rescue, as evidenced by the massive outpouring of help to find Leiby once it became apparent he had gone missing. As the facts of the kidnapping unfolded and the facets of this horrifying tragedy became clear, did it seem to some that God Himself had gone missing as well?

# CHAPTER 4

# DO WE HATE EVIL?

There are six things the Lord hates, seven that are detestable to him: haughty eyes, a lying tongue, hands that shed innocent blood, a heart that devises wicked schemes, feet that are quick to rush into evil, a false witness who pours out lies and a person who stirs up conflict in the community. *(Proverbs 6:16-19)*

To fear the Lord is to hate evil; I hate pride and arrogance, evil behavior and perverse speech. *(Proverbs 8:13)*

Let those who love the Lord hate evil… *(Psalms 97:10)*

Early Christians like Paul embraced the Jewish Bible but rejected what they called the "vengeful" God of the Old Testament. In His place they gave us Jesus, a deity who they said was synonymous with love. Whereas the Hebrew God of Israel says explicitly, "I have loved Jacob, but Esau I have hated" (Malachi 1:2–3), with the former representative of those who strive for peace and the latter a symbol of those who live by the sword, Jesus says in the New Testament that one must love even one's enemies and turn the other cheek to an attack, seemingly advocating passivity in the face of blind cruelty.

But is this what Jesus himself really meant? He never said "Love *God's* enemies." God's enemies are the religious police in Saudi Arabia that allow young girls to be burned alive in their high school rather than flee the inferno without a face covering. Jesus said, "Love *your* enemies." Your enemy is the guy who got promoted over you at work, the driver who cut you off in traffic and nearly caused an accident, or the guy who steals your parking space.

If a terrorist were to succeed, God forbid, in blowing up New York City, by "turn the other cheek" did Jesus intend for us to let this terrorist destroy Los Angeles as well? Or was Jesus instructing us that when a friend does something inconsiderate or says something unpleasant about us, we should try to transcend the provocation rather than bear a grudge? It seems to me any other understanding of this statement makes a mockery of one of the greatest moral teachers of all time.

Jesus, as I explain in my book *Kosher Jesus*, hated the Romans for their cruelty. Luke 13:1–2 describes the brutality of the Roman proconsul Pilate, which Jesus used as an illustration for his students. "Now there were some present at that time who told Jesus about the Galileans whose blood Pilate had mixed with their sacrifices. Jesus answered, 'Do you think that these Galileans were worse sinners than all the other Galileans because they suffered this way?'"

In my book *Kosher Jesus*, I argue against the sanitized interpretation of Jesus, the Jewish rebel against Rome put to death by the empire for opposing Caesar. The effects of this gross misapprehension have implications that are felt till today for the genocidal behaviors commonplace in the twentieth century. How did the world allow such suffering? Could it have been perhaps because we practice love without hate, which means we sometimes lack the motivation to stop monsters from committing their crimes against innocents?

Are we surprised when the Chinese president is given only the second state dinner of the Obama presidency while his government brutalized the reigning winner of the Nobel Peace

Prize? Or when Obama had to be compelled by the British and French to oppose Gaddafi with force? Or Obama's next-to-nothing-but-rhetoric stance to save the citizens of Syria from the hands of the murderous Bashar Assad?

Were we appalled when the Carter administration lobbied to have the mass-murdering Khmer Rouge recognized in the UN as the legitimate government of Cambodia? Or when Kofi Annan, at the time head of UN peacekeeping forces worldwide, forbade the commander of the UN peacekeeping force in Kigali to use force to stop the Rwandan genocide? Annan would later be rewarded for his inaction and lack of abhorrence for grand-scale slaughter by becoming UN secretary-general.

Can love exist without hate? Can someone claim to love the one and a half million children killed by Hitler without hating the SS that gassed them and dashed their brains against rocks? When my friend Professor Jonathan Webber took me on a tour of Tarnow, Poland, he escorted me to a clearing in the woods to see a mass grave of some three hundred orphans who would not stand still when the SS tried to shoot them. So the order went out to slam their heads against a tree that he showed me. Am I supposed to love the monsters that could practice such savagery against helpless children? Can you love the eight hundred thousand innocent Tutsis, savagely cut up with machetes in Rwanda, without hating the Hutu brutes who just a few hours earlier had been their friends and neighbors? Can you claim to love peaceful protesters in Tehran while refusing to hate the tyrant Ahmadinejad who mowed them down in the streets in the summer of 2009? And can you love the victims of Pan Am 103 without hating a murderous Gaddafi for raining down their bodies over Lockerbie?

*Is the greatest challenge to our belief in God and His goodness perhaps not His apparent silence in the face of human misery but our own?*

The most celebrated people in history are those who defeated wickedness and hated evil. Those who appeased it are remembered in infamy.

But how many times have we heard that the problem with the world today is that there isn't enough love? *Isn't the precise opposite true? Doesn't evil stalk the earth because we don't hate it enough to fight it and eradicate it?* Today, even moral people, people with a solid commitment to ethics and religion, are afraid to hate because they think of hatred as a poison that will get into their system and ruin them. And instead, their unwillingness to hate is making them indifferent to evil.

Humankind has entered the third Christian millennium, but evil has yet to be subdued. Seventy years after Hitler, miniatures of the monster-madman run countries; gas their own people; torture men, women, and children; and fill mass graves with the bodies of innocent citizens. Since the world's protests of "Never again a Holocaust" and the UN ratification of the treaty against genocide back in 1948, no fewer than four genocides have taken place. Two million Cambodians killed by the Khmer Rouge, eight hundred thousand Tutsis at the hands of machete-wielding Hutus in Rwanda, hundreds of thousands of Bosnian Muslims by ethnic-cleansing Serbs, and at least a hundred thousand poor black Christians at the hands of the Islamic Janjaweed militias in the Sudan.

Even these numbers pale in comparison to the nearly four million Africans killed in the civil war in Congo. Then we have the estimated 3.5 million North Koreans starved to death under the regime of Kim Jong-il. When he died in December 2012, the United Nations ordered all flags at its global offices flown at half-staff to mourn the mass murderer who took the food of nearly a million murdered children to give to his army instead.

How could this happen in so sophisticated an age, you ask? Could it be that murder and mayhem continue because humanity

– not God – does so little to stop them? Humanity has made great strides in conquering distance, disease, and destitution. So why not evil? Why have we failed at purging the world of awful people and awful actions?

Perhaps the modern approach to evil can be summed up in a famous photo published on the front page of the *Sun* in the UK, and the *New York Post*, featuring Saddam Hussein in his underwear. Even the millions of people who supported the Iraq war found the photograph of Saddam in his skivvies funny. The Butcher of Baghdad in his briefs. But there was nothing funny about it. Shouldn't the image of a man who killed more than a million people – tens of thousands with poison gas – evoke such revulsion within us that it becomes impossible to laugh? Shouldn't nausea, rather than giggles, be our instinctive response?

Jokes about evil people are the norm today. *Saturday Night Live* routinely ran skits featuring Saddam Hussein talking to Osama bin Laden, and everybody chuckled. This is not a question of whether such humor is in poor taste. It's a question of our prevailing human instincts. How can we find skits involving a diabolical murderer like Osama bin Laden entertaining? Can a man laugh if he is gagging on a piece of bread? No. But he can laugh at a murderer if his instinctive abhorrence for murder has been overridden.

Is evil running rampant not because of God's failure to intervene but because the good people of the world opt to focus on difficult-if-not-impossible-to-achieve redemption and rehabilitation? Is their refusal to hate weakening their commitment to fighting what is wicked in our world?

How do we know when it's no longer enough just to hate the crimes? How do we know when we must start to "hate the sinner," too? God, Who can read hearts and souls, may detect real repentance and therefore forgive a dastardly murderer. But isn't that a role best left to Him, and isn't it our duty to punish this destroyer of life instead? Do we really want to live in a world where a mass murderer like Anders Behring Breivik can take the lives of seventy-seven people, most of them teenagers, and be sentenced to a measly twenty-one years in prison?

The ancient rabbis of the Talmud explain that when Moses, in a moment of supreme divine grace, said to God, "I beseech You to show me Your glory" (Exodus 33:18), the core of his request rested on the question "Why, oh God, do the righteous suffer while the wicked prosper?" (*Berakhot* 7a). Moses was saying that the essence of God cannot be fathomed without first knowing why it is that good people are subjected to torment and affliction.

Without an adequate response to this question, our knowledge of God is clouded by the confusion of presumption. To simply overlook our perception that God remains seemingly indifferent to the pain of billions of decent people is to establish a deeply dishonest relationship with Him. The most fundamental of religious questions remains: How can we worship God if we aren't convinced that He is just? If we are to believe there is a God Who cares and is attentive to our prayers, what of the prayers of the six million Jews He allowed to perish in gas chambers? Or those of the parents of children with Tay-Sachs and other terminal genetic diseases who beg daily for divine intervention that does not come? What of Leiby Kletzky's prayers?

Every other spiritual question pales in comparison. While religion has managed to survive the various intellectual "isms" of the last century (Darwinism, Communism, Freudianism, and biblical criticism, to name but a few), the greatest challenge to religion remains the need to rebuild the bridge between the silent God and the suffering masses. If we do not address this mother of all religious questions adequately, religion becomes a sham, a lie, a flimsy bill of goods that offers superficial comfort at best, and added pain at worst.

We need not go on endlessly with more tales of tragedy and woe; I trust you will agree with me that the history of the world is a history of war, persecution, natural disasters, disease, early fatalities, and unspeakable crimes perpetrated by the mighty against the defenseless. What we don't know is why the world is this way, and how we are supposed to endure such grief, time and again, year after year, without turning our backs on God in bitterness and anger.

# PART II

# WHEN POWERLESS GODS HAPPEN TO GOOD PEOPLE

CHAPTER 5

# RABBI KUSHNER'S INTERPRETATION
# OF JOB

Have mercy on us, Lord, have mercy on us, for we have
endured no end of contempt. *(Psalms 123:3)*

For the Lord is good; His lovingkindness is everlasting
and His faithfulness to all generations. *(Psalms 100:5)*

In 1981, in a groundbreaking publishing debut, Rabbi Harold
Kushner wrote the international best seller *When Bad Things
Happen to Good People*. Its effects were mesmerizing. In the
introduction, Rabbi Kushner wrote that when he was a young
congregational rabbi, inexperienced with the process of grief, he
would visit people suffering from a debilitating illness or tragic
loss and rarely wonder about God's justice. He did not question
God's fairness. He simply assumed God knew more about the
world than he did.

He fully bought into the traditional notion of God as the "all-
wise, all-powerful parent figure who...would protect us from
being hurt or from hurting ourselves, and would see to it that
we got what we deserved in life."[1] By the same token, he believed

---

1   Harold S. Kushner, *When Bad Things Happen to Good People* (New York:
    Anchor Books, 2004 [originally published by Schocken Books, 1981]), 5.

in the concept of reward and punishment. "If we were obedient and deserving, [God] would reward us. If we got out of line, He would discipline us, reluctantly but firmly."[2] Certainly it felt easy and natural to believe in such a God when one felt rewarded with health and a good life.

But Rabbi Kushner's faith was loaded with a time bomb set to detonate when tragedy struck close to home – destroying all he had come to know and rely on in terms of the way the world should work. The rabbi's son, Aaron, was diagnosed with the rare accelerated-aging disease progeria, from which he would ultimately die at the age of fourteen.

Rabbi Kushner had been a devoted congregational rabbi, who had done much to alleviate the suffering of others. Rather than pursue a life of unbridled materialism, he had become a spiritual shepherd who selflessly attended his flock. *What could he and his wife have done to deserve such devastation and loss?* Moreover, what had his son done to deserve this fate?

Even the patriarch Abraham, called upon to sacrifice Isaac, was ordered by God to stay his hand at the last moment. His son was returned to him alive. God had no desire for Abraham to suffer the loss of his beloved child. On the contrary, the boy's life was spared and Abraham was rewarded for his loyalty. What kind of sadistic test was God now inflicting on another faithful servant?

In order to understand God's role in human suffering, Rabbi Kushner felt his entire theological basis had to be reconfigured. He needed an understanding of God that would accommodate – not explain away – both large-scale tragedy (like the Holocaust) and his own personal tragedy. In addition, he wanted a relationship with God that fostered worship out of love and admiration rather

---

2   Kushner, *When Bad Things*, 5.

than duty or fear. And finally, he needed a God for whom he could feel respect, not anger. Given all that he and his wife and his son had gone through, this was no easy set of goals to achieve.

Like anyone who has suffered an irretrievable loss, Rabbi Kushner began searching for the answer to the inevitable *why me?* However, unlike others whose introspection may steer them to the depths of despair and loneliness, Rabbi Kushner's quest led him to the pages of the Bible. He began his theological reconstruction with the quintessential classic on suffering, the book of Job. In all of the world's apocalyptic literature, no story comes closer to capturing the existential drama that suffering evokes: the initial rage against God, the inadequate comfort rendered by Job's friends, the searing soul-searching on the part of a devastated Job, and finally, the hope and restoration that suffering may bring about.

What Rabbi Kushner famously came to understand in his rereading of the text was that there are three axioms we all wish to uphold in our understanding of the workings of the world:

- First, that God is all-powerful.
- Second, that God is good (He rewards the just and punishes the wicked).
- Third, that humanity (represented by Job) is good.

Job, like Rabbi Kushner and like most of us, was able to accept all three axioms when everything was going smoothly in life. Indeed, it is easy to believe that through His omniscience and omnipresence, God regulates every happening in our world and provides bountiful goodness and blessings to all. However, once predators and beasts begin to roam the earth, once the innocent begin to suffer at the hands of tyrants, once incurable disease ravages the vulnerable bodies of the righteous, we are forced to reexamine these three axioms and dispose of the pieces that do not fit the puzzle.

The devastation visited upon Job is near total:

> One day when Job's sons and daughters were feasting and drinking wine at the oldest brother's house, a messenger came to Job and said, "The oxen were plowing and the donkeys were grazing nearby, and the Sabeans attacked and made off with them. They put the servants to the sword, and I am the only one who has escaped to tell you!"
>
> While he was still speaking, another messenger came and said, "The fire of God fell from the heavens and burned up the sheep and the servants, and I am the only one who has escaped to tell you!"
>
> While he was still speaking, another messenger came and said, "The Chaldeans formed three raiding parties and swept down on your camels and made off with them. They put the servants to the sword; and I am the only one who has escaped to tell you!"
>
> While he was still speaking, yet another messenger came and said, "Your sons and daughters were feasting and drinking wine at the oldest brother's house, when suddenly a mighty wind swept in from the desert and struck the four corners of the house. It collapsed on them and they are dead; and I am the only one who has escaped to tell you!" (Job 1:13–19)

> So Satan went out from the presence of the Lord and afflicted Job with painful sores from the soles of his foot to the crown of his head. Then Job took a piece of broken pottery and scraped himself with it as he sat among the ashes. (Job 2:7–8)

Amid these seemingly unfair, unjust, and devastating afflictions, Job's friends come to comfort him. Some comfort they provide! Rather than easing his pain, they increase it by offering rationalizations for his suffering, justifications for the blows that have befallen him. They are God-fearing men and hold fast to the first two axioms – their belief in God's omnipotence and their faith in His goodness – for fear that their world and all the principles upon which it is built will otherwise disintegrate.

For them, as for most of us, it is far easier to dispose of axiom number 3, Job's goodness. If such terrible things are happening to him, surely it is because he is a bad person. So they admonish Job to search his heart and evaluate his actions. If he goes through his life with a fine-tooth comb he will discover he has received exactly what he deserves. The calamity that has befallen him is just punishment for his iniquity. In essence they tell him, *Job, you're indignant about your suffering because in your mind you are righteous and believe you've done nothing to warrant such annihilating punishment. But you're surely overlooking something, because* **God would never have afflicted you if your slate were clean.** *You're the guilty party. God is blameless.*

## CHAPTER 6

# WE GET WHAT WE DESERVE

---

Blessed is the one whom God corrects; so do not despise the discipline of the Almighty. For he wounds, but he also binds up; he injures, but his hands also heal. From six calamities he will rescue you; in seven no harm will touch you. In famine he will deliver you from death, and in battle from the stroke of the sword.... "We have examined this, and it is true. So hear it and apply it to yourself." *(Job 5:17–20, 27)*

---

The "blame the victim" response is a reflex manifest by theologians of all religions and denominations throughout the ages. Why do people suffer? Because they are sinful. They deserve everything they get. And if they themselves do not warrant the affliction, then their parents earned it, or their grandparents. And if their lineage has been righteous for generations, then it is the community that deserves it and the righteous must often suffer for the sake of their flock. But one way or another, God does not torment the innocent. God is just. God is good. God is loving. God is innocent. It is *man* who is culpable and thus responsible for the suffering that befalls him.

In a striking case in point, my longtime debating partner on the subject of Judaism, Christianity, and Jesus, my friend Dr. Michael

Brown, the Jewish-Christian scholar and missionary, writes in his book *Answering Jewish Objections to Jesus*, "In terms of those who never heard about Jesus, we believe that virtually all of them are in a fallen, lost state.... There is no question that our responsibility as children of the one true God is to tell everyone that there is a judgment, there is a hell...and there is a way of escape: Jesus the Messiah has paid for our sins."[1]

Dr. Brown also speaks of Noah, and the punishment heaped upon humanity by God in the ancient story. "When the flood came in Noah's day, only eight people were spared.... You had better make sure you know how to receive forgiveness of sins and how to live a life that the Lord Almighty accepts. This is nothing to take lightly."[2]

Of the disasters rampant in today's world, and our seemingly dismal state of affairs, he explains, "There are two other factors that should also be considered relative to human suffering in our day. First, God is beginning to judge the world for centuries of sin and disobedience, and the earth itself is vomiting out its inhabitants."[3]

And finally, in direct reference to the suffering of Jews throughout history, Dr. Brown writes, "There is something important we must recognize, even though it is terribly painful even to consider. From a biblical perspective, the most common reason Jewish blood has been shed is that we Jews have strayed from God, violated his covenant, broken his laws, and failed to heed his prophets.... Let me take this one step further and ask you an even more difficult question: What if Jesus really was our Messiah and we were given a choice to receive him or reject him?

---

1   Michael L. Brown, *Answering Jewish Objections to Jesus: General and Historical Objections* (Grand Rapids, MI: Baker Books, 2000), 33.
2   Ibid., 55, 56.
3   Ibid., 94–95.

What would be the consequences of our saying no to our God-sent deliverer?"[4]

Sin, Dr. Brown tells us, is the cause of suffering. People get what they deserve. God is always just. And thus, those (aka we Jews) who have rejected God's gift, Jesus, are suffering as a result.

Dr. Brown is not alone in his belief that God will punish the sins of man. One unforgettable example of a religious leader's belief in this divine system of checks and balances came to the world's attention following the September 11 attacks. In an incident that sent every media outlet and news publication into a frenzy, Jerry Falwell made the following statement on the September 13, 2001, broadcast of the Christian television program *The 700 Club*: "The ACLU has got to take a lot of blame for this. And I know I'll hear from them for this, but...I really believe that the pagans and the abortionists and the feminists and the gays and the lesbians who are actively trying to make that an alternative lifestyle, the ACLU, People for the American Way, all of them who try to secularize America...I point the thing in their face and say you helped this happen."

Needless to say, many Americans found Falwell's words abhorrent. Some even deemed the speech a hate crime in and of itself. In the wake of the controversy that followed, Falwell attempted to explain his position. "I would never blame any human being except the terrorists, and if I left that impression with gays or lesbians or anyone else, I apologize," he said. Yet, Falwell maintained, "I do believe, as a theologian, based upon many Scriptures and particularly Proverbs 14:23, which says 'living by God's principles promotes a nation to greatness, violating those principles brings a nation to shame,' that the ACLU and other organizations have attempted to secularize America.... I therefore

---

4   Ibid., 102.

believe that that created an environment which possibly has caused God to lift the veil of protection which has allowed no one to attack America on our soil since 1812."

Certainly not the most fulsome apology.

Other conservative Christian leaders had a similar, though less incendiary, response to the attacks. In an interview, *The Early Show*'s Jane Clayson solicited the opinion of Anne Graham Lotz (daughter of Christian leader Billy Graham), stating, "I've heard people say – those who are religious, those who are not – if God is good, how could God let this happen? To that, you say?" Lotz answered, "I say God is also angry when He sees something like this. I would say...for several years now Americans, in a sense, have shaken their fist at God and said, God, we want you out of our schools, our government, our business. We want you out of our marketplace. And God, who is a gentleman, has just quietly backed out of our national and political life, our public life. Removing His hand of blessing and protection." According to Lotz, if God was not actually responsible for this tragic blow to America, He certainly did not shield us from it. And He did not shield us because we no longer deserved to be shielded. Again, we were being punished.

Comments like these have always puzzled me. Firstly, this attitude is so self-incriminating. Does Lotz believe that her father Billy Graham, whom most, including myself, consider a righteous man, has been afflicted with Parkinson's due to sin? Is he, perhaps when we're not looking, really a bad man from whom God has removed His protection?

But aside from the self-incrimination, you have to ask, where is the heart? Are these religious leaders really so callous as to twist the knife into the victims of unspeakable suffering by convincing them that they are themselves responsible for their own pain? And is this not just another insensitive form of "blame the victim"?

Every day I receive e-mails from people communicating their personal problems. They write of broken marriages, children who won't speak to them, parents who have never shown them affection. The tone of anguish in these letters is unmistakable and excruciating. You can feel the pain pouring through the words. The writers want me to figure out how to make the situation right so the pain will go away.

I once tried to respond to the majority of these e-mails. But as the volume increased, I found it difficult to respond to more than a few. Still they would come, and I would peruse them and decide which two or three I would answer.

Then I began to notice something happening as I glanced at these anguished pleas for help. I was no longer feeling the pain of the writers. The personal nature of the e-mails was being lost to me.

Then one day my wife and I had a disagreement over some unimportant detail that mushroomed into an argument. Since I rely on my wife as my closest confidante, I was hurt by the distance it caused between us. I walked away from the argument numb.

I felt lonely and abandoned. I was desperate for someone to pity me. But since fighting with my principal comfort in life – my wife – was the source of my pain, I had no one to turn to for comfort. I agree with the proclamation of the Talmud that without friendship death is better than life. But I did not feel like reaching out to any friends, which only magnified my feelings of despair.

It was at that moment that my mind turned back to all the e-mails I receive. I thought of how I had sometimes closed my heart to strangers seeking my counsel. They were all God's children, each of them precious in His eyes, but I had not found the time to take away their pain. And yet the knowledge that they were out there, and that they, and they alone, understood the depth of my despair, was the only comfort I could find. Strangely, their existence was what sustained me.

I vowed that when I came out of my gloom I would fight with my nature and try to have a more understanding heart and devote myself even more to those in crisis. We all have painful experiences in life and we can all tap into that emotional scar tissue to remind us of our obligation to our suffering fellow man.

Every day of our lives we come across acquaintances, family members, and friends who are in unspeakable emotional pain from domestic strife. But it's a pain that often does not register with us, seeing as it does not involve the death of a spouse or extreme bodily injury. We trivialize this suffering even as the sufferers lose their sanity because they have no *shalom* (peace) in their homes.

Not wanting to be a nuisance to us, they wait for us to inquire as to their dejected state. We indulge them with a light sprinkling of interest by asking a perfunctory question or two, because we do care – just not enough to truly invest ourselves in helping them. And yet alleviating their pain could be as simple as lending a sympathetic ear and an empathetic heart. The most passive effort, like simply nodding acquiescence as they share their trauma, is enough to validate their pain and offer a horizon of hope.

These individuals are not necessarily looking for answers. In many cases, people with significant personal problems already know what they must do to make the situation better. Rather, they need to know that the world is not all pain, that there are people who care and even strangers who see the depth of their anguish.

When I lived in Israel as a yeshivah student I loved and was close to an uncle named David. He nurtured me like a father and loved me like a son. After my two years of study there finished, he lit up like a firework display whenever I would come to Israel to visit.

But then a personal problem began to affect his life. He turned to me for support on my regular visits, but after a while the exposure to a problem I felt I could not help with became a burden. Whenever he brought up the issue, I changed the subject. I came to Israel for inspiration, not depression. So I pretended not to see his distress and I let him down.

A few years later my beloved uncle passed away. He died without my comfort. When we were blessed by God with our third son six years ago, I named him David in my uncle's loving memory. But it was second-tier compensation for a monumental omission. And all I had to do was listen.

In our current state of human development it remains unclear whether we will correct one of life's greatest tragedies, namely, the inability to appreciate a blessing until it is lost.

Somehow we need to go forth as one human family to comfort each other and support one another through pain. If you have a friend who is recently divorced, you have a responsibility to go and offer comfort. If you know a woman whose marriage has ended and who is raising her children alone, give her some support and reassurance. And if you know a man who senselessly argues with his wife or she with him, endeavor to make peace between them.

Yet judgmental words from religious leaders would seek to undermine our responsibility to comfort the suffering and shake our fists at God for human pain. Why, isn't it all our fault anyway? If the person in question were more righteous or virtuous, goes the theory, this wouldn't be happening at all.

So as I sit with people who have tears streaming down their cheeks, should my response be not that I understand the depth of their anguish and that I ask God to alleviate this unjust affliction, but rather that *if only they changed their ways and repented, the pain would go away?*

*This is as sanctimonious, judgmental, and offensive as it gets.* Were I to utter such words I am certain I would not be offering any comfort at all. Moreover I doubt I would ever be invited back.

# CHAPTER 7

# DIVINE JUSTICE AND HUMAN DEFIANCE

Do you not know? Have you not heard? The Lord is the everlasting God, the Creator of the ends of the earth. He will not grow tired or weary, and his understanding no one can fathom. He gives strength to the weary and increases the power of the weak. Even youths grow tired and weary, and young men stumble and fall; but those who hope in the Lord will renew their strength. They will soar on wings like eagles; they will run and not grow weary, they will walk and not be faint. *(Isaiah 40:28–31)*

Hear me, you heavens! Listen, earth! For the Lord has spoken: "I reared children and brought them up, but they have rebelled against me." *(Isaiah 1:2)*

In January 2010, Pat Robertson outraged many when he called the earthquake in Haiti a curse born of the country's historic ties to voodooism. On his *700 Club* TV show he said, "They were under the heel of the French. You know, Napoleon III, or whatever. And they got together and swore a pact to the devil. They said, we will serve you if you'll get us free from the French. True story. And so, the devil said, okay it's a deal."

This pact with the devil is how Robertson explained the devastation that claimed the lives of two hundred thousand Haitians in a single moment as the earth moved. "You know, the Haitians revolted and got themselves free. But ever since they have been cursed by one thing after the other, desperately poor. That island is Hispaniola, is one island. It's cut down the middle. On one side is Haiti, on the other side is the Dominican Republic. Dominican Republic is prosperous, healthy, full of resorts, etc. Haiti is in desperate poverty. Same island. Uh, they need to have, and we need to pray for them, a great turning to God. And out of this tragedy I'm optimistic something good may come." I am friendly with Pat and he has always been very kind to me, as he is to all he meets. I have appeared on his show, *The 700 Club*, numerous times, and he is a consummate Southern gentleman. But one can't help but wonder whether it was some prophecy or voice of God that revealed to him the cause of the Haitian tragedy. And is this what the people of Haiti, who have suffered so much, really need to hear?

In March 2011, Tokyo governor Shintaro Ishihara apologized for saying the tsunami that struck Japan was also divine retribution. Shintaro had originally said the tsunami was needed "to wipe out egoism, which has rusted onto the mentality of Japanese over a long period of time. I think [the disaster] is *tembatsu* (divine punishment), although I feel sorry for all the disaster victims."[1] Was it in a dream that this explanation was revealed to the politician? And given the direct line he has to the One above, one wonders why he stopped at elected office when he could have proclaimed himself a global prophet.

---

1   Cited in Devin Dwyer, "Divine Retribution? Japan Quake, Tsunami Resurface God Debate," ABC News, March 18, 2011.

The same sentiment had earlier been echoed by Reverend David Yonggi Cho, senior pastor of the Yoido Full Gospel Church in South Korea, the largest church in the world. Cho was quoted throughout the world media as having said that the tsunami was "God's warning.... Japan sees a lot of earthquakes, and I think it is regrettable that there has been such an enormous loss of property and life due to the earthquake. Because the Japanese people shun God in terms of their faith and follow idol worship, atheism, and materialism, it makes me wonder if this was not God's warning to them."

In 2007, in his foreword to Lawson's *Foundations of Grace*, John MacArthur writes:

God defines for us what justice is, because He is by nature just and righteous, and what He does reflects that nature. His free will – and nothing else – is behind His justice. This means that whatever He wills is just; and it is just, not by any external standard of justice, but simply because He wills it.

Because the justice of God is an outflow of His character, it is not subject to fallen human assumptions of what justice should be. The Creator owes nothing to the creature, not even what He is graciously pleased to give. God does not act out of obligation or compulsion, but out of His own independent prerogative. That is what it means to be God. And because He is God, His freely determined actions are intrinsically right and perfect.

To say that election [defined by MacArthur as "the fact that God chooses (or elects) to do everything that He does in whatever way He sees fit"] is unfair is not only inaccurate, it fails to recognize the very essence of true fairness. That which is fair, right, and just is that which God wills to do. Thus, if God wills to choose those whom He will save, it is inherently fair for Him to do so. We cannot impose our own ideas of fairness onto our understanding of God's working. Instead, we must go to the Scriptures to see how God Himself, in his perfect righteousness, decides to act.[2]

Indeed, the most central Christian belief is that we are all "fallen," born in sin, and that sin was transmitted from the first man, Adam, to all his progeny. Likewise, Christ died for the sins of humanity and brings about collective absolution for anyone who believes in him. He was the sacrifice whose blood atoned for human sin. He was the slaughtered lamb whose blood expiated the sins of all people throughout time, so that today humanity lives in a state of grace and man has no basis for a claim against God.

At least according to some.

And yet, MacArthur's words seem not only absurd but deeply ignorant. For it is not *we* who are imposing on God a manufactured idea of fairness. Rather, *it is God Himself* Who revealed to us – in a Bible that religious Christians like MacArthur consider divine – the definition of fairness. God commands us to treat all workers fairly and pay them what we owe them on the same day. "'Do not defraud or rob your neighbor. Do not hold back the wages of a hired worker overnight'" (Leviticus 19:13). Is it therefore acceptable for Him to send tsunamis and earthquakes against us that destroy all the accumulated wealth we require to feed our families? Is that fair?

Just three verses later in the same chapter of Leviticus it famously says, "Do not stand idly by the blood of your neighbor." Is it fair of God, then, to watch silently while fifteen thousand Jews are gassed every day for a period of four years during the Holocaust?

---

2   John MacArthur, foreword, in Steven J. Lawson, *Foundations of Grace: A Long Line of Godly Men* (Reformation Trust Publishing, 2006), 9.

God also says famously, "Do not take advantage of a widow or an orphan" (Exodus 22:22). Yet Who made them widows and orphans in the first place? *Who is the one really taking advantage here, the dishonest landlord who will bilk a poor widow, or the God Who seemingly robbed her of her husband in the first place?*

When we challenge God to practice justice, rewarding the innocent and punishing the guilty, we are not superimposing our ideas of right and wrong on the Creator. To the contrary, He Himself commands us, "Justice, justice shall you pursue" (Deuteronomy 16:20), implying, through the repetition, that not only the ends but the means must be just. When we decry the taking of a life, we do so based on God's teaching that life is all that is blessed, while death and murder are something that we are expressly forbidden from participating in. These are not our values but God's.

While the religious faithful may be prepared to bow their heads before God's judgment in silence and willingly accept being cursed for their misdeeds, Job will have none of it. He is utterly defiant. He rejects this rationale. No matter what he's told, he knows that though he may not be perfect, he has done nothing to merit such retribution. He also knows, based on what God has revealed to him about the rules of fairness, that he, a righteous man, has been treated unfairly. Job is not prepared to relinquish his belief in his *own* righteousness because he knows his actions and his heart. He rejects the idea that he is born in sin or that compared to God all are sinful or that all somehow fall short. For God to create humanity to be judged by some impossibly high mark of perfection would itself be grossly unjust and unfair. And God is righteous and God is just. In a just universe, nothing Job has done could have invited such devastating repercussions.

If I have sinned, what have I done to you, you who see everything we do? Why have you made me your target?

Have I become a burden to you? Why do you not pardon my offenses and forgive my sins? For I will soon lie down in the dust; you will search for me, but I will be no more. (Job 7:20–21)

Nor is Job willing to sacrifice the first axiom of his faith, namely, belief in God's omnipotence. Job is no fool. His eyes have seen the glory of God's awesome power. He is far too moved by the wonder of the universe – by the twinkling of the stars, the majesty of nature's peaks, the infinite expanse of the cosmos, and the soaring sweep of the eagle – to accept that anything in the universe is outside of God's control.

His wisdom is profound, his power is vast. Who has resisted him and come out unscathed? He moves mountains without their knowing it and overturns them in his anger. He shakes the earth from its place and makes its pillars tremble. He speaks to the sun and it does not shine; he seals off the light of the stars. He alone stretches out the heavens and treads on the waves of the sea. He is the Maker of the Bear and Orion, the Pleiades and the constellations of the south. He performs wonders that cannot be fathomed, miracles that cannot be counted. (Job 9:4–10)

Rather, Job chooses to dispose of Rabbi Kushner's second principle. He challenges God's goodness. Job concludes that God is so mighty that He is not limited by considerations of justice and fairness. Indeed, if He limited Himself to the dictates of morality and ethics, He would be a limited God. And if He were a limited God, then he wouldn't be God at all. Job rails and thunders against a God Who has abandoned him, against a God Who evinces no mercy, against a God Who plays with man as He would a puppet, pulling and contorting him to His own satisfaction and folly.

Your hands shaped me and made me. Will you now turn and destroy me? Remember that you molded me like clay. Will you now turn me to dust again? Did you not pour me out like milk and curdle me like cheese, clothe me with skin and flesh and knit me together with bones and sinews? You gave me life and showed me kindness, and in your providence watched over my spirit. But this is what you concealed in your heart, and I know that this was in your mind: If I sinned, you would be watching me and would not let my offense go unpunished. If I am guilty – woe to me! Even if I am innocent, I cannot lift my head, for I am full of shame and drowned in my affliction. If I hold my head high, you stalk me like a lion and again display your awesome power against me. You bring new witnesses against me and increase your anger toward me; your forces come against me wave upon wave. Why then did you bring me out of the womb? I wish I had died before any eye saw me. If only I had never come into being, or had been carried straight from the womb to the grave! Are not my few days almost over? Turn away from me so I can have a moment's joy. (Job 10:8–20)

Like Job, Rabbi Kushner was unwilling to surrender his belief in his own goodness to make sense of his suffering. He describes himself and his wife as honest, God-fearing people who, in their chosen pastoral role, always attended to the needs of their community in Massachusetts. While they were subject to human flaws, they were good and loving people committed to God and to their faith. There could be no justification for God striking down their son.

He writes, "It didn't make sense. I had been a good person. I had tried to do what is right in the sight of God.... I believed that I was following God's ways and doing His work."[3] However, unlike Job, Rabbi Kushner was not willing to deny God's goodness. He felt God without goodness was an abomination, however awesome His power might be. He could not believe in, and certainly not trust, God if He were not good. More importantly, as Kushner says, if God is not committed to justice and kindness as we understand it, if He is "so powerful that He doesn't have to be fair," then from where would we draw our own morality? And why would we want to worship Him?[4] Goodness, for Rabbi Kushner, is God's very essence, the divine core. And it is nonnegotiable.

God's omnipotence, however, was less important to Kushner. While God's supremacy is also a central tenet of the Bible, Rabbi Kushner realized he could live with a God Who might not be all powerful, so long as He was all good. Thus, in choosing to abandon that first tenet, Kushner broke, some would say boldly and heretically, with millennia of Jewish tradition by miniaturizing God.

The belief in God's goodness is a central tenet of the Bible. In that pivotal moment just after the children of Israel commit the sin of the golden calf, Moses asks God to reveal His very essence – and God shares with Moses His thirteen attributes of mercy.

> And [the Lord] passed in front of Moses, proclaiming, "The Lord, the Lord, the compassionate and gracious God, slow to anger, abounding in love and faithfulness, maintaining love to thousands, and forgiving wickedness, rebellion and sin. Yet he does not leave the guilty unpunished; he punishes the children and their children for the sin of the parents to the third and fourth generation." (Exodus 34:6–7)

---

3   Kushner, *When Bad Things*, 4.
4   Ibid., 48.

Yes, God commits to punishing those who are guilty of sin and transgression in that passage. But first He promises to be a fair and just judge. This idea is repeated in Deuteronomy.

> But it was because the Lord loved you and kept the oath he swore to your ancestors that he brought you out with a mighty hand and redeemed you from the land of slavery, from the power of Pharaoh king of Egypt. Know therefore that the Lord your God is God; he is the faithful God, keeping his covenant of love to a thousand generations of those who love him and keep his commandments. But those who hate him he will repay to their face by destruction; he will not be slow to repay to their face those who hate him. Therefore, take care to follow the commands, decrees and laws I give you today. (Deuteronomy 7:8–11)

Rabbi Kushner was unwilling to dispose either of God's goodness or man's, and thus he had no choice but to dismiss God's omnipotence. Therefore, Kushner, a traditional rabbi, arrived at a decidedly nontraditional idea: Not everything that transpires in the world is God's will. God's power has limits.

## CHAPTER 8

# A WEAKENED, ABSENTEE GOD?

---

Lord, you have been our dwelling place throughout all generations. Before the mountains were born or you brought forth the whole world, from everlasting to everlasting you are God. You turn people back to dust, saying, "Return to dust, you mortals." A thousand years in your sight are like a day that has just gone by, or like a watch in the night. Yet you sweep people away in the sleep of death – they are like the new grass of the morning. *(Psalms 90:1–5)*

How long, Lord, will you look on? Rescue me from their ravages, my precious life from these lions. I will give you thanks in the great assembly; among the throngs I will praise you. *(Psalms 35:17–18)*

---

How can God be God if He is not all-powerful? Is Rabbi Kushner serious about offering us a God Who can't save us from cancer? Should we buy into a God Who cannot perform miracles when they are needed?

Truth be told, had Rabbi Kushner's book not become one of the most influential books of the twentieth century, I would never have believed people could embrace so limited a God. But millions of people found comfort in the Kushnerian deity, even though He was such a fundamental departure from the God they had encountered in Sunday school.

In Rabbi Kushner's premise, God *is* completely loving. He cares enormously about ordinary people and human suffering. He is attuned to the pain and plight of His children. But God is unable to intervene when it comes to the laws of nature and human free choice. As Rabbi Kushner says, although God may grieve and wish things turned out differently, "it is too difficult even for God to keep cruelty and chaos from claiming their innocent victims."[1] Later, he writes, "Neither...can we ask God to change laws of nature for our benefit, to make fatal conditions less fatal or to change the inexorable course of an illness.... Sometimes miracles do happen.... [But] we don't know why...."[2]

Rabbi Kushner maintains that once God put the laws of nature into motion they became fixed and immutable. As a result, gravity works democratically for all. It does not suspend or change if we are righteous or sinful. If an airplane develops engine trouble and falls out of the sky, murderers and adulterers, as well as saintly figures and innocent infants, are incinerated in the crash. In other words, the direction of nature's wrath is not in any way guided by morality. This is actually a new form of *neo-deism*, a belief that God started it all by creating the world but then left everything to run by itself, as sort of an absentee landlord. Natural law itself is divinely ordained, and God never interferes with His already established order.

The second area where God's power is limited, according to Kushner, is the arena of human moral freedom. This means that once God gave mankind the freedom to choose between good and evil, He could no longer stop the bullet when someone decided

---

1  Kushner, *When Bad Things*, 49.
2  Ibid., 128–29.

to murder. Protecting the innocent would be an abrogation of moral freedom – something God simply cannot allow. Therefore, if we want to do terrible things, "God will not reach down and pull our hand away from the cookie jar."[3] God will warn us what is wrong. God will inspire teachers to tell us what is wrong. God will arrange the world so we will suffer the consequences of doing what is wrong. But the bottom line is that if we are insistent on doing wrong, we are free to do so because "if we are not free to choose evil, then we are not free to choose good either."[4]

In Kushner's view there is no true goodness in the world without freedom of choice. Hence, in the name of goodness, paradoxically, God withdraws from the realm of human decision making totally and absolutely. Consequently, He cannot forestall the progress of the Nazis into Poland any more than He can upend the rules of morality itself.

So then, what good is this Kushnerian God? Why would any of us be attentive to a God incapable of upholding goodness and preventing evil? Rabbi Kushner responds to these questions by emphasizing that his severely limited God is not to be viewed as a mere bystander. On the contrary, Rabbi Kushner finds proof of God's existence in the ability of the human mind to respond with compassion and to try to solve the problems that plague humanity: "Isn't my feeling of compassion for the afflicted just a reflection of the compassion He feels when He sees the suffering of His creatures?"[5] He sees human activity that promotes the betterment of the world and the alleviation of suffering as divinely inspired: "God inspires people to help other people who have been hurt by life.... God makes some people want to become

---

3   Ibid., *When Bad Things*, 90.
4   Ibid., 89.
5   Ibid., 156.

doctors and nurses.... God moves people to want to be medical researchers, to focus their intelligence and energy on the causes and possible cures for some of life's tragedies."[6]

Rabbi Kushner also sees God as the One Who helps ease our suffering. God accomplishes this by sending us caregivers to nurse us and care for us when we are ill. He sends us friends and family to grieve with us when we mourn. He sends spiritual leaders to guide us with their vision, and inspires writers to comfort us with their words and brilliant artists to remind us that there is always beauty and exquisiteness in the world.

Finally, Rabbi Kushner sees the presence of God in the ability of ordinary people to do extraordinary things. How else, he says, can we explain the phenomenon that occurs when people act with superhuman strength and courage at times of extreme circumstances? How can we explain the talents of an athlete or an artist or a mathematician that seem to surpass what we otherwise knew to be humanly possible? How do we account for the "unbelievable" accomplishments achieved by humanity, if it is not God Himself at work, channeled through the human vessel?

Kushner's ideas of God are alluring because they allow us to "maintain our own self-respect and sense of goodness without having to feel that God has judged us and condemned us."[7] Moreover, "instead of feeling that we are opposed to God, we can feel that our indignation is God's anger at unfairness working through us, that when we cry out, we are still on God's side, and He is still on ours." Though Kushner has, in effect, severely weakened God by removing cruelty (which is the result of human free choice) and chaos (the result of natural laws) from the realm of His control, he has at the same time vindicated Him. Indeed,

---

6 Ibid., 153.
7 Ibid., 51.

Kushner actually *saved* God from the masses that harbor hostility toward Him by proposing a God that not only grieves for us when we suffer but is ultimately blameless when it comes to our anguish.

By removing all culpability from God as the agent of human suffering, Kushner offers us a God that is the source of comfort rather than castigation, reassurance rather than retribution, and pleasantness rather than punishment.

But is this really so? Many questions remain. Principle among them: *If God is so utterly limited that He can't, for example, prevent cancer, and we instead have to rely on doctors alone to treat us, why do we need God at all?*

# CHAPTER 9

# A CHILD'S KNOWLEDGE OF PAIN

In my distress I called to the Lord; I cried to my God for help.
From his temple he heard my voice; my cry came before him,
into his ears. *(Psalms 18:6)*

We wait in hope for the Lord; he is our help and our shield.
In him our hearts rejoice, for we trust in his holy name. May
your unfailing love be with us, Lord, even as we put our hope
in you. *(Psalms 33:20–22)*

For you have been my hope, Sovereign Lord, my confidence
since my youth. *(Psalms 71:5)*

When I was eight years old, I faced the harsh reality of my parents'
separation, and later divorce, a bitter end to a troubled and
turbulent marriage. To this day, their divorce holds distinction as
the most pivotal trial of my early life – the event that triggered my
preoccupation with the imperfections of the world and my desire
to repair them. I was a child often lost in thought; my parents' split
devastated and confused me further. My father's absence after my
mother, brothers, sisters, and I moved from Los Angeles to Miami
exacerbated feelings of displacement. A rather fatalistic view of
the world took hold and became embedded in my personality.

But it wasn't until I attended summer sleepaway camp at age nine that I realized how different I was from other kids. Each night when our counselor announced "lights out," my bunkmates would put up token resistance, but within five minutes of their head hitting the pillow all the boys were fast asleep – except me. I would lie there in the darkness, eyes wide open, envying my bunkmates who slept so soundly while I tossed and turned. Finally, I brought my problem to our head counselor, who smiled at me and said, "Those boys have nothing to think about. Why should they stay awake? But you? You're trying to make sense of the world, so you can't fall asleep." He meant to flatter me, but to my ears, his words just confirmed my feelings of abnormality.

I knew that compared to kids with cancer or to homeless kids with empty stomachs every day, my trials hardly constituted suffering. I understood how lucky I was to have a mother and father who loved me, even if from opposite sides of the continent, and siblings I was close to. But I still felt cheated. My mother worked two jobs to support her five children and often got home late at night. We lived in a one-bedroom apartment, where my brother and I slept in the living room. The building itself was awash with dysfunctional families and even violence, and on April Fool's Day 1976 a police officer was shot to death before my very eyes.

The melancholy of my childhood abated somewhat when my grandparents provided the down payment for a house in a pretty middle-class neighborhood in Miami Beach and helped with the tuition to send us to a Jewish day school. Though money was tight and we could afford none of the "extras" my friends took for granted, it was the emotional poverty that devastated me. I couldn't help staring at dad-and-son pairings as they walked down the street together. The annual synagogue-sponsored father-son softball game had me waiting on the sidelines with my mitt, hoping to be picked for a team even though my dad wasn't there.

Once a year, my brothers and I would travel to Los Angeles to spend Passover with my father. It was wonderful to be with him. But then we would have to leave and I was again left dangling, an emotional yo-yo bobbing aimlessly between two homes and two parents. After years of attending Hasidic summer camp, I grew committed to the Chabad movement. I traveled almost nightly to their local yeshivah to study. The more time I spent in yeshivah, the greater sense of comfort I found in God. Every night I prayed to Him with a fervor that even today I would find difficult to duplicate. Feeling God's presence was soothing and reassuring. I felt He understood my sadness and listened when I cried.

At fourteen, I took a big step. I left home to study full-time in yeshivah in Los Angeles. The move had an additional perk: Although I lived in the dorm, I now saw my father nearly every Sunday, when he would drive to the school to visit me. It was during these yeshivah years that Rabbi Kushner's book first came to my attention. While few in the Orthodox Jewish world took notice of it – and those who did dismissed it as heretical and philosophically unsound – I was intrigued.

Despite my piqued interest, I did not have occasion to read the book until I was twenty-two. Then, as rabbi at Oxford University in England, I found myself counseling students who had experienced tragedy. I began having strong ideas about the authentic Jewish response to suffering and decided to write a full-length work that would address the issue from a Jewish mystical perspective. One of the first things I did was to go to Blackwell's, Oxford's world-famous bookstore, to buy a copy of Rabbi Kushner's book.

I finished reading the slim volume in one Sabbath afternoon. Two realizations came to me immediately. The first was that the book's diminishment of God's power was off-putting. Rabbi Kushner offered a God radically different from the One I had encountered in all the Bible's miracles. I didn't see the point to praying to an impotent God Who did not control the world. The second impression: *Kushner could not simply be dismissed for a number of reasons, not the least of which was that he came across as a moral giant,* a man whom God had endowed with tremendous gifts for empathy and compassion, not to mention one of the most lucid and accessible writing styles I had ever encountered.

While I found the book theologically objectionable, I understood why so many millions had found it so comforting and liberating.

# CHAPTER 10

# WHAT RABBI KUSHNER GOT RIGHT – AND WHY I DISAGREE

---

"For I know the plans I have for you," declares the Lord, "plans to prosper you and not to harm you, plans to give you hope and a future." *(Jeremiah 29:11)*

You, Lord, hear the desire of the afflicted; you encourage them, and you listen to their cry. *(Psalms 10:17)*

But the eyes of the Lord are on those who fear him, on those whose hope is in his unfailing love. *(Psalms 33:18)*

The Lord is close to the brokenhearted and saves those who are crushed in spirit. *(Psalms 34:18)*

---

Amazingly, Rabbi Kushner had emerged from the loss of his beloved son with a message of hope and promise. A man who had endured such an unspeakable tragedy, remarkably, refrained from bitterness. He and his God were at peace. Thus, while I could not agree with the ideas expressed in the rabbi's book I found Rabbi Kushner himself to be extraordinarily compelling.

For one thing, I was inspired by his argument that as human beings, we are obligated to dedicate ourselves to the alleviation of suffering. As the Bible instructs, we may not "stand idly by the blood of [our] neighbor" (Leviticus 19:16), and we must "love [our] neighbor as [our]self" (Leviticus 19:18). Rabbi Kushner writes, "How does God make a difference in our lives if He neither kills nor cures? God inspires people to help other people who have been hurt by life, and by helping them, they protect them from the danger of feeling alone, abandoned, or judged."

Thus, even the atheist scientist who applies his intelligence to finding a cure for disease is doing more to expedite God's work than the clergyman that asks us to embrace our suffering for the character it builds – or worse, tells us that we deserve it for our sins. This Kushnerian supposition resonated deeply with me.

In addition, I admired Rabbi Kushner not only for his unquestionable courage regarding his son's illness, but also for his willingness to challenge tradition. All the cliché explanations about suffering to date had been ineffectual at best, offensive and inflammatory at worst. Indeed, I was deeply repulsed by speeches and essays that "blamed the victim" and maintained God was "the great blackmailer in the sky" (a phrase I first heard from atheist Oxford philosopher Jonathan Glover, during a debate I organized at the university between him and my friend Dennis Prager), Who spent His time pouring fire and brimstone on errant humans.

This repulsion became especially acute when it came to the Holocaust. In the second half of the last century, some Orthodox Jewish thinkers had declared the Holocaust divine retribution for Jewish abandonment of tradition. Rabbi Joel Teitelbaum, the Satmar Rebbe, felt that the Holocaust was a punishment for secular Zionism. Jews should not have begun moving en masse to Israel before God redeemed them Himself, and thus the Holocaust was divine retribution for the chutzpah of Zionism.

Rabbi Menachem Hartom, an Israeli theorist, said rather that it was precisely Jewish abandonment of Zionism that provoked the communal punishment of the Holocaust. Once Jews began to enjoy the benefits of post-Enlightenment assimilation, they no longer yearned for Zion, and for this anti-Zionism they incurred Gods' wrath.

The more I read ideas like these, the more alienated I felt. Were these religious thinkers seriously suggesting that the punishment for Jewish assimilation was being tortured, starved, and turned into ashes by the millions? Were they doing God or His people any kind of justice by portraying Him as a vindictive tyrant? Would anyone want to worship a God guilty of such monumental devastation for a lack of religious obedience? And was a God Who could do this even worthy of prayer? Upon the publication of Kushner's book, many Orthodox Jewish scholars castigated his minimization of God as being completely contrary to tradition. But were their explanations really any more authentic?

I felt strongly that Rabbi Kushner had led the way in affirming the rights of man in the face of seeming divine injustice. And I agreed with Rabbi Kushner on one major point: Judaism could no longer offer shallow rationalizations for pain or explanations that always made man responsible for his own suffering.

I turned to the source for solutions. I pored over the Bible, looking for a consistency in how the giants of Jewish history dealt with the trials of suffering. The more I read, the more I realized their response was to challenge God rather than to implicate man. When the great biblical heroes, figures like Abraham and Moses, were confronted by the anguish of their contemporaries, they took action to absolve man and charge God, rather than the reverse.

Armed with this knowledge, and despite my admiration for Kushner's courage and originality, I began to feel his approach was another form of apologetics. While some rabbis let God off the hook by asserting that mankind brought suffering upon itself, wasn't Rabbi Kushner letting God off the hook by declaring He had no control over the bad things that happen in this world?

Miniaturizing God was, in the final analysis, another form of exoneration. Like the many enthusiasts of *When Bad Things Happen to Good People*, I found Rabbi Kushner's book well reasoned, beautifully written, and rich with deep humanitarian insight. I was taken with Rabbi Kushner's enormous compassion, and moved by the comfort he sought to extend to his struggling readers. But having pondered his words over many weeks, I finally concluded his thesis bore not only terminal theological flaws but logical ones as well. Moreover, I surmised the comfort afforded by the book was ephemeral and somewhat misleading.

To those in pain as a result of feeling abandoned by God, Rabbi Kushner's remedy came in the form of a virtual *denial* of God. The new, diminished God proffered by Kushner seemed not pitiable, but pathetic. How are we to find comfort in a diminutive God, powerless to help the innocent when what we need is for Him to intervene? Shouldn't we be placing our hope in and addressing our prayers to a God that can actually assist? Would a Jew stricken with typhus in Auschwitz, who has just experienced the destruction of his family, his community, and all that he holds dear, really benefit from knowing that a God lacking the power to intercede feels his sorrow?

*People cry out to God because He is Lord and Master of the universe, not because He sheds tears as people die.* Take the families of the thirty American soldiers killed August 2, 2011, while aboard a helicopter rushing to aid troops in a firefight – would it have been any comfort to them to know, for example, that the governor of the Bahamas, or some other remote and powerless onlooker, felt sorry for them? Or that he had monitored their suffering closely but could do nothing to assist them?

There is sometimes little comfort in comfort alone. Indeed, when someone in a position to end our suffering comes to console us after the fact, we don't feel comfort – we feel contempt. We resent the silence of the passive onlooker, who observed with sympathetic eyes but never intervened. In the final analysis, just how innocent is an innocent bystander after all?

In his haunting book, *The Town beyond the Wall*, Elie Wiesel introduces us to Michael, a teenage survivor of the Holocaust. The entire narrative focuses on Michael's return to his little Hungarian village to confront the gentile neighbor who watched but did nothing while Michael's family was deported. At the end of the book, it becomes evident that the "neighbor" being pursued is God, the real "silent One."

Could Kushner explain away a God Who stood by and watched as millions upon millions of Jews were slaughtered? Would he reason that God couldn't have done anything to help, since He was powerless Himself? But wouldn't this make God only more culpable? If you're a powerless God, then why did You ever hold out false hope? Why did You allow us to believe there was a moral order at work in the universe, which ultimately ensures the righteous flourish and the wicked are punished? While Kushner's God does not appear to be immoral, the case could be made that He is *amoral*. Kushner's God is as silent and passive as nature itself. Who among us believes that praying to nature will net positive results?

Notwithstanding how compelling and truly comforting Rabbi Kushner's arguments were, I concluded his theories were seriously flawed. What Rabbi Kushner was offering us was the deist's concept of God – a God that creates the universe, installs the laws of nature, but then ultimately leaves the world to operate according to its own devices. This makes God into something akin to a deadbeat dad. He created vulnerable humans and then left them to fend for themselves, without making sure to be around to intervene if necessary to protect and guide them. Wouldn't we have just cause to be deeply disappointed with, or even despise, such a God?

*Honey, I created cancer...now deal with it.*

It also struck me that whereas the Bible declares in one of its most famous pronouncements that God created man in His own image (Genesis 1:27), Kushner had reversed the process. Echoing a quote thrown around with atheistic irony in the 1960s – "On the eighth day *Man created God*" – Kushner was creating God in the image of man.

Kushner's God was warm, wise and cuddly – a grandfather figure filled with compassion, but ultimately feeble and powerless. I myself had no use for a God with limits on His power. After all, who needs a God perched up in the heavens unable to intervene in the affairs of humankind? Isn't praying to such a deity little more than wasted breath? Therefore, despite the phenomenal respect I felt (and feel) for Rabbi Kushner, who would later become a friend and mentor, I was quite certain his ideas had to be contested. It took three years of study and contemplation to write my own book on suffering, *Wrestling with the Divine: A Jewish Response to Suffering*, asserting my rebuttal to Kushner's perspective and elucidating my personal views.

It surprised me that no one had beat me to the task. Rabbi Kushner had opened a gaping hole in millennia-old Jewish, Christian, and Islamic theology, and on the subject of God Himself, no less. He had done so in an earth-shattering way with a hugely successful and influential book. How was it possible that no one else had endeavored to refute the man who had convinced millions that God was good but ultimately powerless? Was I the only one troubled by this suggestion?

In *Wrestling* I argued that once we've exhausted our human resources to try to end suffering, our response must be to "wrestle with the Divine." It is our obligation as humans to challenge God and hold Him accountable. Unlike Islam, which translates literally to "submission to the will of God," and Christianity, which advocates acquiescence and faith as religion's highest callings, I called attention to the fact that the very definition of the word *Israel* means "He who wrestles with God." I countered that rather than inspiring man to stand up and fight for what's right, religion had emasculated man by telling him he had no right to question God at all. I insisted that **challenging God and His actions is not just our right, but our foremost obligation as human beings.**

# PART III

# A NEW-OLD APPROACH

## CHAPTER 11

# PROFESSIONAL WRESTLERS: ABRAHAM, MOSES, AND LEVI YITZCHOK

---

This day I call the heavens and the earth as witnesses against you that I have set before you life and death, blessings and curses. Now choose life, so that you and your children may live and that you may love the Lord your God, listen to his voice, and hold fast to him. For the Lord is your life, and he will give you many years... *(Deuteronomy 30:19–20)*

---

In rebuttal to those who argue that challenging God is sacrilege, I ask, what does Abraham do when God threatens to destroy Sodom and Gomorrah? Even though God had said, "The outcry against Sodom and Gomorrah is so great and their sin so grievous that I will go down and see if what they have done is as bad as the outcry that has reached me" (Genesis 18:20–21), Abraham pounds his fist and demands justice for them from the Creator: "Will not the Judge of all the earth do right?" (Genesis 18:25). Abraham's challenge to God – and in such strong, direct language – staggers the imagination. The Bible itself had established the depravity of the people of Sodom. One imagines God saying, *It's a well-considered and deserved fate, Abraham. I know what I'm doing, okay?*

How dare Abraham interfere? And worse, how dare Abraham come so close to accusing God of injustice? Does any human being have the right to stand in the face of the Creator of heaven and earth and accuse Him of being unjust? Abraham takes up the cudgel and becomes the world's first great defense attorney. And defend humanity Abraham does, despite its culpability, because it is his obligation as a fellow creature on this earth. The people of Sodom are, after all, his human brothers and sisters. And it is his responsibility to do everything in his power to save their lives, even if that means opposing God. Indeed, Abraham pleads with the Judge of the world to show mercy upon all of His creatures.

The same is true of the prophet Moses. How does the great redeemer react when God threatens to destroy the children of Israel after the debacle of the golden calf? Does he bow his head in submission before the will of God? Does he simply accept God's justice? God says to him, *Look here, I delivered the Jews from slavery, wreaked havoc on the Egyptians to accomplish this, and now here they are, just a few weeks later, trading Me in for a hunk of metal. This is just not right. The people have proven themselves unworthy. They will be immolated, and you will become the father of a greater nation in their place. You will be like Romulus and George Washington, not just a prophet, but the father of a new people.*

And at this point, with a darn good offer on the table, Moses, in one of the most haunting and moving passages of the Bible and one of the most eloquent defenses of human life ever recorded, says to God, "But now, please forgive their sin – but if not, then blot me out of the book you have written" (Exodus 32:32). The book he is referring to is the Bible, of course. Moses demands, should God fail to find it within Himself to forgive the people, that He strike the name Moses from the Bible altogether – thus severing their relationship forever, with Moses departing the faith community – if God can be so callous. Where in the annals of any apocalyptic literature do we have a prophet challenging God in this manner? One gets goose bumps just reading the passage.

Moses had monumental chutzpah. In essence, he said, *I don't want to be associated with a God capable of such cruelty.* And of course God is *not* that kind of God, and never wishes to be. The Talmud (*Berakhot* 32a) points out that before issuing the threat, God prodded Moses to intervene. "And now *let me be*, Moses, so I may destroy them."[1] Let me be? Moses hasn't said anything. But God was admonishing him, goading him. *Here I am discussing the destruction of human life and you are sitting there silently. Your role is to object. You are never to accept seeming divine miscarriages of justice, Moses. I am God. I give life and I take life. That is my prerogative. But you are human and you are not to concern yourself with death. Don't try to figure out My higher plan. Your objective is to always cherish life, promote life, and defend life.*

The Bible is clear: "The secret things belong to the Lord our God, but the things revealed belong to us and to our children forever, that we may follow all the words of this law" (Deuteronomy 29:29). God is in charge of the hidden things. Why does He allow humans to suffer unjustifiably? What are His concealed reasons? That is none of our business as humans. What goes on in secret behind the partition of heaven is of no human concern. The revealed things, however – these are our business. A person is suffering right before our eyes. A parent is mourning the death of a child. A woman is crying over the loss of her husband and life partner. Why did they die? For no reason at all. Their suffering served no higher purpose. The death is in no way redemptive. It is, by

---

1   The Talmud points out that God uses these words also after the incident of the golden calf: "Now leave me alone so that my anger may burn against them and that I may destroy them" (Exodus 32:10). Were these words not found in the Torah itself, the Talmud says, it would not be possible to infer them here.

everything God has revealed to us about the beauty of life and its infinite value, a bad thing, something that has to be corrected and reversed. We are not here to understand why God takes life. As far as we know, it happens for no reason at all. It should not happen. The death of innocents is ugly, it is destructive, it is bad, and it is wrong. Tragedy and misfortune are incompatible with a God Who proclaims He loves life. So we must protest against His taking of life. Like Abraham and Moses before us, we must never surrender.

*In the face of suffering, each and every one of us must not exonerate God but rather demand clemency for man.* We have to stick up for each other, even if it means defying God. God is the Father of humanity. Like any parent He loves His children more than Himself. He would rather we assail Him than each other. He wants us to stick up for one another. The reason He so loved great individuals like Abraham and Moses was because they defied Him when they saw God's children suffering and demanded that it stop. It was in the merit of a profound love of humanity, and a preparedness to protest against God in its service, that both Abraham and Moses merit to become fathers themselves. Abraham, a father of a nation, and Moses, the father of a faith. Only those with true parental feelings can be parents to the human family.

The most honest and useful response to suffering is not to rationalize human agony or to accommodate human grief, but to make every effort to obliterate both from the face of the earth.

The time has come to end the misconception that suffering exists either to punish human sin or ennoble human character. To the contrary, suffering is the very enemy of life. Any good that could come our way as a result of suffering could just as easily have come about without suffering. If we do happen to become better people after we have been through a painful episode, the gains made are *despite* the fact that we suffered, not because of it. The correct response to suffering is to wage an unrelenting war against it until suffering is purged from the earth. Part of that war is never to dignify it with any kind of explanation. If suffering happens for a reason, if pain serves some purpose, then both occupy a vital place in our world. But if they are utterly senseless, if they serve no purpose whatsoever, then the only thing left to do is purge them utterly from our world. And that is humanity's first obligation. As Jews say thrice daily in their prayers, our responsibility is "to repair the world under the kingship of God." No world is perfect if there is even a trace of suffering. So let us never dignify it with an explanation again.

Vulnerable human beings who bleed when stabbed and endure agony when bereaved need all the help we can offer. But religion has made the terrible error of casting itself in the role of God's defender and of pain's protector, when its primary obligation should be as *man's* defender and pain's obliterator. Like Abraham and Moses before us, we must shake the heavens and implore God not to provide us with comfort but to keep the promises He made to our forefathers for a good and bountiful life.

If that means taking on God, so be it. It is our religious duty to do so. We should follow the example set by Rabbi Levi Yitzchok of Berdichev (1740–1809), one of the most popular and beloved figures in modern Jewish history. Born into a prominent rabbinical family, he was a noted scholar and spiritual leader. Rabbi Levi Yitzchok served a number of Polish communities in the late eighteenth century. After meeting rabbis Shmelke Nikolsburg and Dov Ber of Mezeritch, he was won over to Hasidism and eventually became one of its most influential leaders. He is particularly famous for defending the Jewish people before God and always interpreting their actions in the best possible light. Once he saw a Jew praying with his *tallis* and *tefillin*, the morning religious ritual objects, while saddling his horse. Rabbi Levi Yitzchok's *shamash* (assistant) immediately criticized the man for desecrating prayer and his *tefillin* by not allocating adequate time and place for prayer. But rather than find anything untoward in the man, Rabbi Levi Yitzchok exclaimed, "Look, Lord. Even when Jews *work* they pray. Even when they do something as mundane as saddling their horses, their thoughts are turned to You."

Rabbi Levi Yitzchok was a shining example of the Jewish principle of wrestling with the divine in the service of human innocence. Jews who speak of him proudly call him a defender of Israel, saying, "When we remember the Berdichev rabbi, the strictness of heaven's justice softens." They speak of his prayer, in which the rabbi would challenge God directly: "I, Levi Yitzchok, the son of Sarah from Berdichev, have come to have a trial with You on behalf of Israel, Your people."

There are a great number of colorful stories illustrating the rabbi's constant debating with God in defense of the human race. Legend has it that one year, when Rosh Hashanah began on the Sabbath, Rabbi Levi Yitzchok prayed as follows before his congregation: "Heavenly Father! Today, on the anniversary of the day when You created the world, You will judge all its creatures for the coming year. Some You will judge favorably, and You will write their names in the Book of Life. Others have committed various grave sins, and You will, God forbid, inscribe them in the Book of Death. Yet today is the Sabbath, and have we not learned in Your holy Torah, oh Master of the universe, that one may not desecrate the holiness of the Sabbath by writing? Yet your Torah is a Torah of life, as it is said, "Keep my decrees and laws, for the person who obeys them will live by them" (Leviticus 18:5). You therefore decreed in Your infinite wisdom that it is permitted to violate the laws of the Sabbath for the purpose of saving a life, and it is thus permissible to write today in the Book of Life. Yet an inscription in the Book of Death is completely contrary to the spirit of Your holy Sabbath and is utterly forbidden today! Accordingly, Heavenly Father, there is only one choice: all of Your creatures must be inscribed today only for good, for a year of life, blessing, and wealth!"

Yet another apocryphal story relates that on Yom Kippur, the holy day of atonement, the entire congregation waited as Rabbi Levi Yitzchok seemed enraptured in thought. As the people grew impatient on the fast day, he finally told the congregation to sit down and related to them, "Holy brothers, I have just had a conversation with God. He told me that many of us had sinned and justice demanded consequences. I responded, 'But Master of the universe, in what did they sin? Slander, sexual immorality, violation of the Sabbath? However, no one in this community made a woman a widow this year. But You did, oh Lord. And no one in this community made any child an orphan. But You did, oh Lord. And no one brought famine and pestilence to any other party this year. But You did, oh Lord. Forgive us our small sins and we will forgive You Your great ones."

# CHAPTER 12

# A JEWISH APPROACH TO THE GREATEST OF ALL QUESTIONS

---

But with righteousness he will judge the needy, with justice he will give decisions for the poor of the earth. He will strike the earth with the rod of his mouth; with the breath of his lips he will slay the wicked. *(Isaiah 11:4)*

For God will bring every deed into judgment, including every hidden thing, whether it is good or evil. *(Ecclesiastes 12:14)*

---

A lengthy dispute took place between the Talmudic academies of Hillel and Shammai in the first century. The two great seats of learning debated whether it is better for man to exist or never to have been created at all. They argued the issue for a lengthy period of time, and while disagreeing on a host of legal and philosophical issues, on one thing they both agreed: it would have been better for man *not* to have been created (*Eruvin* 13b).

Even now in the modern world, after medical breakthroughs and the establishment of communication capabilities that unite so much of our globe, life is still riddled with tragedy, isolation, and hate; financial, emotional, and political instabilities. Overwhelmed by the uncertainty of it all, who among us has not stopped watching the news or reading the newspaper, beleaguered by the challenges that haunt our very existence?

Life is not arbitrary. Existence is not meaningless. People shouldn't be expected to trade their loved ones for any amount of comfort that friends, relatives, and even God Himself can provide. Comfort is only an intermediary step that at best centers us so we can fight the mother of all battles: the war against suffering itself.

Human beings have a right to demand a good life from our Creator. In fact, we have an *obligation* to do so. We should demand from God that we be able to go to work in the morning in a downtown office building to support our families and to come home safe and sound. When our loved ones are crushed beneath thousands of tons of concrete, God is not doing His job. When they are forced to make a choice between burning to death and dying as the result of a fall from thousands of feet in the sky, God is not doing His job.

Just as God rightfully makes demands of us – that we be good and decent, honest and devoted, generous and open-handed – we, too, have demands, and *life* is foremost among them. Telling people to remain silent in the face of suffering encourages them to have a dishonest relationship with God, a relationship of restrained feelings and hidden emotions, repressed rage and latent anger. Clerics should be calling first and foremost for people to practice a living faith, one that includes the right to make demands of the Creator, and to respond with appropriate anger and indignation to the suffering He permits. That may sound odd. But what is the alternative? A fraudulent relationship where we are but cosmic chaff who must endure brutal and painful suffering while singing songs of praise to God through our agony? Would God want that kind of tinny, robotic response from the warm-hearted humans He created?

When Elie Wiesel watched six million innocents be incinerated in Hitler's ovens, it kindled his anger at God and he wrote haunting books and made daring speeches that shook the heavens in protest. Humans were not cosmic chaff that had to simply accept God's judgment. Before Wiesel, many people of faith had a fake relationship with the Creator, one governed by humble resignation rather than bold affirmation. Whenever humans were faced with tragedy, they were expected to bow their heads in silent submission. But through Wiesel was reborn the ancient – and lost – Jewish tradition of wrestling and sparring with God. It is Wiesel's insistence on the rightful place of the individual within the God-man relationship that allows for the possibility of intimacy within that relationship.

This is what I am advocating: a wholesome, holistic relationship with God that gives Him full credit for the good that is in our life at the same time that we feel aggrieved when bad things happen, God forbid. This actually strengthens our faith because it shows that we accept that everything comes from God and that our relationship with Him is real, all-encompassing, and complete.

Rabbi Kushner wanted to deflate our anger at God. He wanted us to be reconciled with God and to understand that, while God loves us, He is helpless to rescue us. Not only do I disagree entirely with the God Kushner fashions, I disagree that this anger is something unholy. Our rage against suffering is essential, it is righteous, it is sacred. *Our righteous indignation against an all-powerful deity who is seemingly silent while children die is something He Himself demands.* It was God Who taught us that death and suffering are bad. In the Torah He commands us to "choose life" and to abhor death. He commands us to alleviate the suffering of all we meet – even our enemy's animals: "If you see the donkey of someone who hates you fallen down under its load, do not leave it there; be sure you help them with it" (Exodus 23:5).

So surely He would never expect us to overlook suffering or excuse it. Our refusal to come to terms with the world's imperfections is paramount. God's accountability must not be surrendered at any cost.

Indeed, God demands no less, as we see from His interaction with Noah. After the great flood and the destruction of life on the earth, Noah and his family leave the ark unharmed. The Midrash tells us that Noah, after seeing all the destruction, cries out to God and asks, "Lord, how could You have destroyed all these people?" God responds to him, "Why are you asking Me this now? You were one of the few righteous people on earth, and it was in your power to save them. Yet you did not utter one voice of complaint or prayer when I told you they were all destined for destruction."[1]

God was telling Noah that had he prayed and pleaded with Him, asking for fairness and mercy, God would have listened to these prayers to put off the flood and given the world more time to repent. Yet the moment Noah was told that he and his family would be safe, he had nothing more to say about the matter. God therefore told Noah that he had failed one of his major missions in life by not getting agitated and arguing with God over humanity's fate. Clearly God wants people to argue and plead for the lives of even the wicked, that they may become good: "Why will you die, people of Israel?" God exhorts the people in Ezekiel 33:11. "For I take no pleasure in the death of anyone, declares the Sovereign Lord. Repent and live!"

God wants us to demand the moment of consolation when "he will swallow up death forever. The Sovereign Lord will wipe away the tears from all faces" (Isaiah 25:8).

Throughout rabbinic literature, we find an interesting concept known as "l'hatiach devarim k'lapei ma'alah," which translates literally, "casting words towards heaven." It involves arguing with God and even, so it would seem, speaking harshly to Him when

---

1   My translation from *Zohar Chadash* 254.

we see others suffering, or when our own suffering becomes unbearable. Abraham, Moses, Elijah, Hannah, Job, Habakkuk, Jonah, and Mordechai are some of the figures in the Bible described as arguing with God in an attempt to prevent an evil decree from happening to others. Each one faced a unique challenge and used different avenues of debate and argumentation to try to bring a pardon and forgiveness. Sometimes it worked and God relented, and sometimes God said that nothing could be done, yet even so these great personalities continued to plead and contend with God to change His will. This practice continued with the great rabbis in the Talmud, and throughout the exile, even to our very generation today. We can learn from their examples for our own prayers to God.

A perfect example of this concept is the story of Choni the Circle Drawer. He lived in the generation preceding Herod and was known for his outstanding piety. The Talmud recounts how there was a drought in the land of Israel and the fasting and prayers of the community were not helping. The people reached out to Choni and asked him to pray for them. He prayed to God yet no rain fell. The Mishnah in *Ta'anit* 23a describes:

> He marked out a circle around himself and said: "Creator of the universe! Your children have always looked up to me as being like a son of Your house. I swear therefore, by Your great Name, that I will not move from this place until You have compassion upon Your children." Whereupon it began to drizzle. "It was not for this I prayed," said Choni, "but for rain sufficient to fill the wells, cisterns, and caves." The rain then fell in torrents, each drop as large as the mouth of a barrel. "Not for such rains have I prayed," said Choni, "but for mild, pleasant, and plentiful showers." The rain then fell in the usual manner, until the Israelites of Jerusalem were

obliged to seek refuge from the city to the Temple Mount on account of the rain.

They then came to him and said: "Rabbi, even as you prayed that the rain might fall, pray now that it may cease." And he replied: "I have a tradition that it is not permitted to pray for a cessation of too much good. Still, bring me a praise offering." It was accordingly brought to him, and putting both hands upon it, he said: "Creator of the universe! Your people that You brought out of Egypt cannot be sustained either with too much evil or too much good. When You became angry with them, they could no longer bear it; and now that You have showered too much good (rain) upon them, they cannot bear it either. Let it be Your will that the rains may cease and the world become happy." Thereupon a wind came up, dispersed the clouds, the sun commenced to shine, and the people went out into the fields and brought back mushrooms.

According to the great twelfth-century Jewish sage Maimonides, we are required to pray every day, asking God for our needs. If we need something in life, we are obligated to God to ask for it. And because we are all children of the Almighty, we must beseech God as Choni did. We must have the audacity to ask God as many times as necessary for what we need. If we see that God has not fully met our needs, we must tell Him that this is not what we have been praying for. And if He gives us too much blessing, we must ask that He give it in a way we can handle in life. In *Avot d'Rebbe Natan* we learn that when Miriam spoke ill of Moses and contracted leprosy, Moses drew a circle around himself and told God he would not budge until Miriam was healed.

The only correct response to suffering is to dedicate our every effort to its obliteration, thus creating a world that will welcome in the Messiah and a more perfect world. Some will see this as unrealistic. My response is to remind them of the beautiful quote from Robert Browning's poem "Andrea del Sarto": "Ah, but a man's reach should exceed his grasp – or what's a heaven for?" Making peace with suffering shows we have no imagination and little spiritual purpose. Preparing elaborate theologies that accommodate death and suffering is the apologetics of spiritual pygmies. We are larger than all that. And so, of course, is God.

Over the years, many traditional critics have assailed me for challenging God. How dare human beings even consider such a proposition! Man is to simply bow his head in submission to the firm belief that everything God does is for the best. Indeed, my critics have served up a host of rabbinical passages that seem to contradict my core thesis.

Invited to lecture on the topic of suffering in the early 1990s in Manchester, England, I was nearly booed out of the hall by the primarily ultra-Orthodox audience. They rallied together and declared my ideas blasphemous. After all, who was I to question what the Master of the universe has in store for His children? It was okay for Abraham and Moses to argue with God: they were the greatest prophets of the Jewish people. But Shmuley Boteach? Letters appeared in the *Manchester Jewish Telegraph*, calling my views "dangerous," "harmful," and "contrary to authentic Jewish values." And that was the nice stuff!

When I included some of my theories about suffering in an essay published on Beliefnet.com in the late nineties, a marginal conservative religious website committed to "converting homosexuals into heterosexuals" published a response to my piece:

Boteach concludes, "I would rather stay awake being angry that God has allowed this [the World Trade Center] devastation to happen, than to sleep easier believing that those who suffered deserved what they got." Shmuley, do you ever sleep? By the way, nobody said that the dead deserved their fate because of the sins of the society. The sins of society cause Divine anger, and that anger is often directed at good people, who are the sacrifices to save everyone else.... In the eternal realm, those murdered in the World Trade Center know why God killed them, and they are content.

Whoa!

A few years later I was invited to address the Jewish community of Hong Kong. I was introduced by the local rabbi and then had the privilege of speaking from the pulpit of the more than one-hundred-year-old Ohel Leah Synagogue. My speech addressed the latest wave of terror bombings against innocent Israeli civilians. I denounced the claim that any of the victims were targets of divine wrath. "This idea," I exclaimed, "is as ridiculous and inaccurate as the repugnant view that held the Holocaust to be punishment for sin. None of us know the actions or the hearts of six million innocent victims. Who among us would be so arrogant as to claim they were deserving of so monstrous a fate? Who among us would condemn 1.5 million utterly innocent children to death for sin? And who among us would so impugn the reputation of God by suggesting that we pray to a deity who could be so callous about innocent human life?"

When my speech came to its close, I greeted many of that evening's attendees. Most of them enjoyed the speech and told me so, but I couldn't help but notice an elderly man sitting in the back – a pious rabbi positively fuming in his solo corner of the synagogue. He made no attempt at diplomacy. "What you said was a disgrace. You are an abomination. How dare you question the authority of the great rabbis who said the Jews of the Holocaust were sinful, and thus were punished? Did you live through that era? No, of course not! You are much too young to know what that time was all about. But I did live through it. I knew many of the victims firsthand, and they got the punishment they deserved. Most of them were ashamed to be Jewish. They lived their lives in constant rebellion against God's laws and thus, they received their comeuppance. And you? You're a *naval birshus Hatorah*, a wretched creature who disgraces the Torah."

As he walked off, I chased after him. "Wait, please, rabbi! Before you go, I really must know! You knew all six million Jews? You knew that they were bereft of merit? You knew they deserved to die?" I called after him. He only turned to hurl more invective at me and continued to walk away.

Those so vociferously condemning my reasoning claim it goes against the grain of Jewish teachings. They cite the many Talmudic quotations that support the idea that there is no suffering without sin. The Talmud says in *Shabbat* 55a: "No death without sin; no suffering without iniquity." They cry from the allegorical rafters that all men are imperfect and sin in some way, as the Talmud says in *Berakhot* 5a: "If a man sees that he is afflicted with suffering, he should examine his deeds, as it is said, 'Let us search and try our ways, and return unto the Lord' (Lamentations 3:40)." The Talmud adds: "Suffering is due to evil deeds or neglect of Torah study." Again in the Talmud *Berakhot* 5a we find: "If he who suffers searches but finds nothing [objectionable], he should attribute his affliction to neglect of the study of Torah."

While some blame the victims for all the evils that are done to them, the sixth Rebbe of Lubavitch, Rabbi Yosef Yitzchak Schneerson, had a different approach. After the Holocaust, as news of the extent of destruction and death were reaching America, journalists in the Jewish community began writing articles claiming that God had broken His covenant with the Jewish people and abandoned them to their fate. An Orthodox

Jewish journalist wrote the sixth Rebbe and asked him if it was a religious requirement to declare war on the authors of these editorials. The Rebbe responded to him, "There are those who are angry with God for all the horrible suffering they have seen. We cannot argue. They have a right. Perhaps God will listen." Clearly, God Himself knows when we are tested beyond our limits, and He understands our pain, disappointment, and even – dare we say it – anger towards Him.

# CHAPTER 13

# IS SUFFERING A BLESSING?

---

For this command is a lamp, this teaching is a light, and correction and instruction are the way to life. *(Proverbs 6:23)*

In you, Lord my God, I put my trust. I trust in you; do not let me be put to shame, nor let my enemies triumph over me. *(Psalms 25:1–2)*

Look down from heaven and see, from your lofty throne, holy and glorious. Where are your zeal and your might? Your tenderness and compassion are withheld from us. But you are our Father… *(Isaiah 63:15–16)*

---

Many statements in rabbinic literature imply that even the righteous suffer for a reason. They maintain a righteous man's suffering serves as atonement for all the people. Midrash Pesikta Zutra states that the Bible describes the death of Miriam right after detailing the laws of the preparation of the red heifer to teach that just as the red heifer atones and cleanses from sins, so does the death of the righteous help cleanse and atone for sin. There are also teachings that the righteous will get their reward in the world to come. Rashi cites in the name of the rabbis that Yaakov wanted to have a quiet, peaceful life when he returned to the land of Israel. But then all the troubles with Joseph came upon him. The righteous wish to live lives of tranquility, but the Almighty responds, "Is it not enough what is prepared for the righteous in the world to come that they also seek to live in peace in this world too?"

Other Talmudic evidence suggests that suffering ennobles our character and refines our spirit. As Rabbi Akiva's students remarked after he was tortured to death for teaching Torah in public, "Blessed are you, Rabbi Akiva, that your life expired with 'Echad' [the final word of the Shema prayer, meaning One, a commitment to the one true God]" (Berakhot 61b). Also in Sanhedrin 101a Rabbi Akiva says, "Suffering is precious." The Mechilta of Rabbi Yishmael (Masekhet d'Chodesh 10) states: "Rabbi Yosef ben Rabbi Yehuda says, 'Precious is suffering since the Lord's name rests on those who suffer for Him.'"

These rabbinic positions, however, derive from aggadah rather than halakhah; in other words, they are narratives rather than legal opinions. Nachmanides says in his famous 1263 debate with Friar Pablo Christiani that we are not limited to or obligated to abide by aggadah. (To demonstrate why he does not believe in the literal truth of a certain aggadah, Nachmanides explains, "We believe in the Talmud concerning explanation of the commandments.") These Talmudic quotes about suffering are aggadot, Talmudic legends. They are not law. They are nonbinding opinions. And they are opinions which, while trying to dignify suffering, seem to run contrary to the biblical model of railing against suffering.

David Birnbaum writes in his excellent book God and Evil that rabbinic writings offer "the concept of yissurin shel ahava, tribulations of love – to purify man, to ennoble man, to chasten man; to raise man to a higher level; to test man; through suffering comes redemption…to provoke man to reflect on his inadequacies and propel man to develop his potentiality…. Suffering keeps man from committing the sin of 'hubris.' Suffering lessens the physical pride and selfish nature of the individual."[1] In defense of this argument, Birnbaum quotes Proverbs 3:12: "the Lord disciplines those he loves, as a father the son he delights in" and Psalms 11:5: "The Lord examines the righteous."

Others opposed to my position that man is obligated to challenge God cite scriptural and Talmudic statements that say finite man cannot understand the infinite God; God's ways are inscrutable; man must have faith in God's justice. Rabbi Yannai said: "We cannot understand the well-being of the wicked nor the suffering of the righteous" (Avot 4:19). Isaiah 55:8–9 relates, "'For my thoughts are not your thoughts, neither are your ways my ways,' declares the Lord. 'As the heavens are higher than the earth, so are my ways higher than your ways and my thoughts [higher] than your thoughts.'" Job 40:2 concedes, "Will one who contends with the Almighty make himself master? He who argues with God, let him answer it." And the Talmud says in *Berakhot* 69b, "As Rav Huna says: 'Whatever the merciful One does, it is for good.'"

These opponents counter my encouragement to rail against life's cruel dealings, saying, "God's ways will be made understandable to us in the next world."

Critics spouted these very same quotes in response to my reaction to the September 11 tragedy. They repeated these passages over and over, in effect asserting we can know nothing now, but we will have all the answers later – therefore, we should not be seeking answers today.

In *Good Omens* (Transworld, 2011), Neil Gaiman and Terry Pratchett offer up a more satirical take based on the famous

---

1   Birnbaum, *God and Evil*, 18.

Einstein quote "God does not play dice with the universe." The authors state: "He plays an ineffable game of His own devising, which might be compared, from the perspective of the players (i.e., everybody) to being involved in an obscure and complex version of poker in a pitch-dark room, with blank cards, for infinite stakes, with a dealer who won't tell you the rules and who smiles all the time."

Is this the lot of mankind? Are we helpless victims groping aimlessly in the dark, struggling to cope with the inscrutable cards we've been dealt by an all-powerful croupier, who never tips his hand in this highest-of-all-stakes game of life?

Or has the time come to definitively challenge the supposition that the suffering of the innocent is due to human sin (that is, they are not really innocent) or that it's a necessary route to breakthroughs in human character? Can we all agree that the most honest and useful response to suffering is not to rationalize human agony or accommodate grief, but to make every effort to obliterate both from the earthly plane? After thousands of years of human history, do we not deserve better from God, and do we not have the right to hold Him accountable, to require of Him that He abide by the same values and teachings that He has imposed upon us? In this unrelenting war against suffering, shouldn't we be committing ourselves to sticking up for one another and demanding mercy for mankind, even if it means defying our Creator? Every parent would hope that strangers would step in to protect their children when they are at risk – is this not what God, our Father in heaven, would want from us as well?

The idea that suffering is redemptive and ennobling is a profoundly Christian idea. If Jesus does not suffer on the cross then mankind is doomed to eternal damnation. Walking into a church and seeing the suffering Christ reminds us that Jesus died for our sins. In Christianity someone dies so that others are redeemed. Christians focus on the bloodletting of Jesus and the suffering of the saints. The very symbol of the Christian faith is Jesus' torment for the sake of mankind. The message is clear: suffering is the route to remission of sin. Moreover, in Christianity no one is really innocent. All are tainted by original sin, the fall of Adam and Eve in the Garden of Eden and its transmission through the human bloodline to all but those who repose faith in Christ.

But Judaism has no such symbol nor any such theology. Precisely the opposite is true. Jews are commanded to end suffering completely and abolish all pain from the earth. The Jewish desire is not to use pain to remit sin and thus gain entry into heaven but rather to end pain, thereby creating heaven on earth.

Are there Jewish sources that suggest that suffering leads to redemption? Yes. My debating partner Dr. Michael Brown loves to quote passages like the following:

"Know then in your heart that as a man disciplines his son, so the Lord your God disciplines you." (Deuteronomy 8:5)

"Blessed is the one you discipline, Lord, the one you teach from your law." (Psalms 94:12)

"Blessed is the one whom God corrects; so do not despise the discipline of the Almighty. For he wounds, but he also binds up; he injures, but his hands also heal." (Job 5:17–18)

Notice that these biblical quotes all come to console an individual who suffers. Here it is important to understand that Judaism distinguishes strongly between the view one takes of oneself and the view one takes of one's fellow man. We all know we're imperfect, and we can all choose to see our suffering (whether we view it as deserved or not) as a corrective experience from which we can learn.

This philosophy also emphasizes the teaching of Nachum Ish Gamzu, who would say when misfortune struck, "This too is for the good" (*Ta'anit* 21a). It is this realization – that whatever happens to us can be looked at in a positive way – that can even allow us to reach a level of feeling outright joy when something bad happens, if only because we believe that someday, somehow, everything will be visibly good and the messianic era will be here.

Of course, it must be emphasized that this only applies to our *own* suffering. When it comes to others, God wants us to feel their pain and get angry over their plight, in order to motivate us to do all we can to help them. Indeed, the originator of the Hasidic movement, the Baal Shem Tov, once castigated one of his disciples for applying this maxim to the pain of others. The Baal Shem Tov had learned that the Jewish community was being forced to house soldiers of the czar, a very dangerous scenario in anti-Semitic Czarist Russia. The Baal Shem Tov approached his disciple Rav Nachman of Horedenka and said they must pray to God to avert this evil decree that was coming to the world. However, Rav Nachman, who would always say, "This too is for the good," responded to the Baal Shem Tov with these same words. The Baal Shem Tov chastened Him: "Thank God you were not around at the time of Haman's decrees to wipe out the Jewish people. Had you been, you would have also replied, 'This too is for the good.'"

When it comes to other people's pain, God wants us to arouse within ourselves a controlled anger about what is happening. That anger must then spur us on to action and prayer.

We have no right to assume another person's suffering is due to sin. We have to assume the righteousness of every person. We have to object to their suffering, as did Abraham, Moses, Rabbi Levi Yitzchok of Berdichev, and others. *While we may choose to accept our own suffering, we must not accept that of others, nor may we come up with theological reasons to justify the suffering of other people.*

Maimonides (the Rambam), born in Cordoba in 1135, stressed this point in his "Epistle on Martyrdom." When Spain was conquered by the Almohad (al-Muwahhidun) Muslims, they sought to convert the Iberian Peninsula's inhabitants – including the Jewish population – to Islam by force. A leading rabbi of the time censured any Jews who, with swords to their necks, uttered the Islamic belief formula, "There is no god but Allah and Muhammad is his prophet." Maimonides turned his encyclopedic knowledge and razor-sharp pen on the rabbi, whom he castigated for condemning Jews who were not prepared to martyr themselves and instead submitted to forcible conversion.

Maimonides quotes from sources all over the Torah to show that those who rebuked the Jews for their sins, or accused them of sin, were themselves severely rebuked and punished by God for attacking His people. Some of Jewish history's greatest figures, including Moses, Elijah, and Isaiah, as well as an angel, spoke against the Jewish people and were punished. How much more so will someone who is not at their exalted level be punished for speaking badly against another Jew?

So if you're going to be talking about the redemptive quality of suffering within a Jewish context, you'd better be talking about your own suffering and not that of others!

I have a simple proof, however, that suffering is not redemptive and that none of us truly believe that it is. For if it were, we would all intentionally inflict suffering on our children. Since we seek what is best for our kids, if we really thought suffering was ennobling, redemptive, and enlightening, we would purposefully inflict suffering on them so that they could benefit from the experience. Moreover, if it were a blessing we would all thank God for our suffering and even pray for it. We would offer praise for suffering and ask for more. Clearly, this is absurd. None of us would ever do any such thing. Not to ourselves and certainly not to our children. We do our utmost to alleviate and prevent suffering, and so we should.

Now, it is true that sometimes children perceive suffering being inflicted upon them by their parents. We do, after all, sometimes deny them things they want, or push them to do things they don't want to do, or even punish them, all in their own best interests and as part of their education. One might argue that God is also our Father in heaven, and He inflicts suffering on us that is just, with our own interests in mind, even though we may not see it. My dear friend Dennis Prager asked me this question: If parents inflict what their children consider to be suffering upon them, but it is really for their benefit, who is to say that what God does is vastly dissimilar? While we may not appreciate it, perhaps what God is doing is indeed for our benefit.

My response is straightforward. We parents do indeed inflict things on our children that may, in their minds, cause them to suffer. Sending them to bed early, depriving them of a favorite toy, taking away their allowance or car keys may seem to them to be grossly unjust punishments. But what we certainly never do to our children (unless we are monsters) is kill them, gas them, tattoo numbers on them, inflict deadly earthquakes and hurricanes on them, starve them to death, give them unclean water to drink, or willfully impart cancer. The idea that we can compare some of the acts of deprivation or slaps on the wrist we inflict on our children to the unbelievable suffering that has regularly befallen innocent humans throughout history is a nonstarter.

Perhaps God will challenge us with a period of financial deprivation, to purge us of materialism. That's painful, but I get it. But a Holocaust? A Crusade? Total financial collapse leading to hunger and homelessness? We as parents might take away our children's iPads; we might not allow them to attend a social function. But no normal human parent causes his child egregious bodily harm – certainly not death or significant deprivation, God forbid. Why wouldn't we insist on the same from our heavenly Parent?

Some might question who I think I am to decide on God's behalf what is fitting and right for Him to do. Certainly I do not have that level of understanding. Rather, I am letting God decide for me. I base my demand on the values God Himself has revealed to us as being blessed: life, compassion, charity.

Over and over throughout the Bible God tells us to live with kindness and compassion for others, and not to harm them:

"Do not do anything that endangers your neighbor's life.... Do not seek revenge or bear a grudge against anyone among your people, but love your neighbor as yourself. I am the Lord." (Leviticus 19:16, 18)

"You shall not murder." (Exodus 20:13)

"Whoever is kind to the poor lends to the Lord, and he will reward them for what they have done." (Proverbs 19:17)

"Speak up for those who cannot speak for themselves, for the rights of all who are destitute. Speak up and judge fairly; defend the rights of the poor and needy." (Proverbs 31:8–9)

"This is what the Lord Almighty said: 'Administer true justice; show mercy and compassion to one another. Do not oppress the widow or the fatherless, the foreigner or the poor. Do not plot evil against each other.'" (Zechariah 7:9–10)

"This is what the Lord says: Do what is just and right. Rescue from the hand of the oppressor the one who has been robbed. Do no wrong or violence to the foreigner, the fatherless or the widow, and do not shed innocent blood in this place." (Jeremiah 22:3)

These are God's instructions for us: this is what He tells us He loves. These values come from Him, not us. Shouldn't we therefore love what He loves, and shouldn't we demand this same behavior of God?

Normal parents would never inflict lasting harm or cruel punishment on their children because parents love their children more than anything in the world. Indeed, most parents, if presented with the knowledge that their children would have to *really* suffer, would willingly invite that suffering upon themselves rather than see it inflicted upon their children.

God is our Father in heaven. We are His children. Surely He feels the same way. And if so, it is incumbent upon Him to show it.

# CHAPTER 14

## LISTENING TO THE REBBE

---

At the time of sacrifice, the prophet Elijah stepped forward and prayed: "Lord, the God of Abraham, Isaac and Israel, let it be known today that you are God in Israel and that I am your servant and have done all these things at your command. Answer me, Lord, answer me, so these people will know that you, Lord, are God, and that you are turning their hearts back again." Then the fire of the Lord fell and burned up the sacrifice, the wood, the stones and the soil, and also licked up the water in the trench. When all the people saw this, they fell prostrate and cried, "The Lord – he is God! The Lord – he is God!" *(I Kings 18:36–39)*

---

All religion is predicated on the idea that God and man share a personal and intimate relationship, and the health of that relationship depends on both parties keeping a number of promises. If we don't keep our end of the bargain, God has the right to be upset with us. But equally binding is God's covenant with us and our obligation to always participate in the affirmation of life – even if such affirmation at times becomes an outright indictment of God. If God chooses to hide while humans suffer, then He opens Himself to the accusations of scoffers that He is indifferent or may not even exist, God forbid.

106

Rather than follow the example of Rabbi Kushner in diminishing God so as to exonerate him, I turned to my own mentor, the Lubavitcher Rebbe, Rabbi Menachem Schneerson, universally and affectionately known as the Rebbe. The Rebbe used love rather than fear, joy rather than guilt, and inspiration rather than criticism to motivate his followers. Even into his nineties, he would lecture to thousands of people every Sabbath. He would pound the table with all the might he could muster. "*How long?*" he would cry, "*How long?*" The point of his question was surely clear to his audience and God alike. How long will young Israeli men and women die in defense of their homeland? Was the Holocaust not enough? Is it a sin for Jews to simply want to live? How long will Jewish history remain tragic? How long will schoolchildren be killed in traffic accidents? How long will disease continue to take loved ones from their families well before their time? How long will parents struggle to simply feed their children?

The Rebbe would demand the arrival of the Messiah. Not request but *demand*. Here was the most famous Jewish spiritual figure of the twentieth century confronting God in front of thousands of people. The Rebbe acknowledged that many great religious authorities claim we lack the righteousness, that we don't deserve the arrival of the Messiah. These leaders had declared our own sins were preventing his coming. But the Rebbe would have none of it. "We have surely earned the right of his arrival!" A more perfect world is something that God owes us. God commands in Deuteronomy 24:15 that one must pay his hired worker the same day. The Chofetz Chaim, a revered Jewish sage of the nineteenth and twentieth centuries, applied this concept to God as our "employer": he wrote in his commentary on the Jewish prayer book that we should demand the Messiah just as a hired worker demands his wages at the end of the day.

The Rebbe would thunder against the heavens, quake against

injustice. We have suffered painfully enough, sacrificed willingly enough, and pleaded long enough. There were no valid excuses. The ball was in God's court, and it was He alone Who had not yet ushered in a perfect world.

When I was a young rabbinical student in Jerusalem in the mid-eighties, a bus filled with schoolchildren was crossing the tracks near Moshav HaBonim when it was hit by a train. Nineteen children and three adults were killed. Rabbi Yitzhak Peretz, the Israeli minister of internal affairs, of the Shas Party, said publicly that Israeli desecration of the Sabbath was responsible for the tragedy.

Rabbi Eliezer Schach, the major Lithuanian rabbi in Israel at the time, regularly echoed these tragedy-results-from-sin sentiments. In December 1990, his view was published in the religious newspaper *Yated Ne'eman* that "God kept count of each and every sin, in a running count over hundreds of years, until the count amounted to six million Jews, and that is how the Holocaust occurred. So must a Jew believe, and if a Jew does not completely believe this, he is a heretic, and if we do not accept this as a punishment then it is as if we don't believe in the Holy One, blessed be He...."

The Rebbe exhorted people in the strongest terms not to lay blame on one's fellow. "People rationalize their instinct to criticize and condemn others by saying it is for the purpose of correcting the other's misdeeds," he said, asserting that the fact that the great prophet Isaiah was punished for criticizing his fellow man proved God wants otherwise.[1] Pounding his fist, he repeated his mantra, which became engraved in the hearts of Jewish followers the world

---

1   From a talk given by the Rebbe on the first of Rosh Chodesh Elul 5742 (August 1982), translated and published by Sichos in English.

over, including myself. "*Ad mosai?*" How long? How long would innocent people suffer? And how long would well-intentioned people excuse it? There was no reason nor rationalization for such tragedy. It served no purpose and it had no legitimate cause. God had simply to stop it.

In February 1992 a woman named Pesha Leah Lapine, a wife and young mother of four, was brutally raped and murdered in Crown Heights, Brooklyn, the Lubavitch world headquarters. Returning from buying groceries near her home, she was attacked and stabbed to death. The murder took place in front of her young children. The next day the Rebbe walked silently as part of her funeral entourage. His face expressed anguish, shock, and horror. On February 13, when the seven days of mourning ended, the Rebbe delivered one of the most memorable and distressing public talks of his life. Mrs. Lapine would not submit to the rape so she was murdered and martyred. She chose this fate in the full knowledge that she would not be present to raise her own children. Even so, she fought with all her strength against being violated. "For a mother this is an even greater act of sacrifice than forfeiting her life."

The Rebbe challenged God in the presence of all his followers. "Enough is enough! Have we not sufficed with all the martyrdom we have experienced until now? …Another day passes, another week passes, another moment passes…and [the Messiah] still has not come. We say and we think and cry out '*Ad mosai!*' How long must we wait in exile?" What powerful words, especially coming from the foremost Jewish spiritual authority in the world. The Rebbe did not let God off the hook. Words and explanations were poor substitutes for the innocent life of a murdered mother. Others could dismiss the Rebbe's optimism about the messianic era as fanciful. But to him it was as real as the table he pounded when he challenged God before the masses.

Judaism's linear tradition begins with creation and culminates in the messianic era. Central to Judaism is a belief in progress. With the advent of every sunrise, we draw closer to that promised era when goodness and plenty will fill the earth. Not only do we wait for that time when "[the Lord] will swallow up death forever" (Isaiah 25:8) and "the wolf will live with the lamb" (Isaiah 11:6), we clamor for it.

According to Jewish thought, God is perfect and His handiwork is potentially faultless. The world's imperfections are God's greatest riddle. Thus, the very purpose of our life must be to help cure these flaws, banish darkness from the earth, and lead humanity into an age of light and brilliance. This is the only strategy I can endorse, the only solution I learned from my Rebbe – a relentless fight against the darkness to usher in the light.

A secular Welsh poet, Dylan Thomas, captured the sentiment beautifully in his famous poem in which he exhorts his dying father to "Rage, rage against the dying of the light."[2]

These ideas and the Jewish concept of messianism are the very engine behind Western civilization and its progress. Messianism introduced the concept of linear history: things begin in an underdeveloped state and get better and better until they near perfection. The world is becoming more wholesome, not less. We are tackling disease, fighting poverty, working on ending war. There are setbacks, of course. But the messianic values that give people the hope that life can be made more perfect are spreading throughout the world and people are expecting more from their lives.

Democracy is spreading, as is a demand for free and open government. Sure, there are setbacks. Too many tyrants and terrorists continue to slaughter innocent people. But by and large, the world is holding them accountable, even if it is not

---

2   Dylan Thomas, "Do Not Go Gentle into That Good Night," 1951.

happening fast enough. This is a radical departure from the idea of cyclical history, proposed by the religions of the East, which do not embrace the idea of historical progress but rather argue that history is destined to repeat itself in never-progressing cycles.

The wheel of time or wheel of history (Kalachakra) is a central idea to many religious traditions and philosophies, especially religions that are of Indian extraction, most notably Hinduism and Buddhism. They regard time as cyclical, consisting of repeating and never-ending epochs. This idea is pervasive in many other cultures who affirm a nearly identical concept. The Hopi Indians of Arizona, the Q'ero Indians of Peru, and many other native American traditions believe in a never-ending cycle of repeated ages.

Judaism rejects this. Long ago the Hebrew prophets foretold of a day when disease would be conquered and death would be defeated. And even though we lose so many valiant fighters along the way, even though new illnesses replace the ones we have eradicated, even though the children tragically lost to sickness today cannot be restored to their bereaved parents, mankind is heading toward a glorious future where freedom from death is attainable.

Sounds crazy, right? But I said these exact words in a *Huffington Post* televised debate against a leading atheist, who likewise dismissed me as a fanciful figure. "Really," I said, "a few hundred years ago a man was lucky to live to thirty-five. Today he lives double and sometimes triple that. We have pushed death pretty far back and must continue to. We must live as if our lives are constant. And if death overtakes us, then at least we will have gone down fighting. But to live in the constant preparation for death is cynical and destructive." By all means, make some rudimentary plans for death. Buy a plot. Have a will. Make provisions for your children. But once that is done, live life to the full and don't reckon with death.

Even the atheist scientist, through dedication to curing disease, is bringing about fulfillment of God's promise made so long ago. And indeed, there are many atheist scientists who are at this moment toiling away at curing AIDS and cancer who are far closer to the Jewish ideal of *Israel*, he who wrestles with God, than many rabbis and priests who are fraudulently telling parents whose children have incurable disease that heaven is a better place than earth.

I've discovered from numerous public appearances that people don't take well to hearing that suffering serves no intrinsic purpose. All who suffer look to find meaning in their pain. We want reassurance that we don't grieve in vain and that our sorrow serves some higher cause. *I agree that none of us suffer pointlessly. But not because suffering has any intrinsic value. Rather, because the pain of suffering spurs us into action to abolish suffering. And that is its purpose.*

As rabbi at the University of Oxford, I hosted Dr. Christiaan Barnard, who in 1967 became the world's most famous surgeon by performing the first heart transplant. I asked him, in the presence of our students, what he was working on now that a shaky hand had made operating difficult. He said, "I am working to cure mankind's most ancient disease." The students asked him, "Do you mean cancer? Or heart disease?" He dismissed their answer. "No, I refer to old age. Why should we just accept," he asked, "that people have to grow old and die? Why do we treat the frailty and incapacity of later years as something inevitable, instead of seeing it for what it is: a disorder that can be cured." You could say he is a madman. But aside from the fact that he was one of the most accomplished doctors of all time, when he arrived in Oxford he was in his seventies, yet he looked at least twenty years younger.

I am sure that to many my ideas here of overcoming suffering or even defeating death are hopeless sentimentalism at best, dangerous delusion at worst. But I submit that all of us have already bought into this belief, whether or not we are aware of it. The belief that mankind can triumph over suffering and rid the world of fatal illness and hunger is part of our everyday life and translates as official government policy in most Western countries.

Over the past decades, many billions of dollars have been thrown at cancer, one of the world's biggest killers, as well as AIDS, a more recent killer. Yet, while we have learned how to halt the progression of each, there is still no cure for either. Why don't we just give up? Why don't we just concede that there are some diseases that cannot be conquered and that death is a part of life? All the money that is being spent on these diseases could be used in a manner that would bring tangible results. We could build more houses. We could give everybody a free college education. Why waste all that hard-earned money on conquering diseases that may have no solution?

By the same token, why don't we make peace with the ravages of nature? Why are we still trying to predict hurricanes and undo earthquakes? In other words, what spurs us, against all the evidence, to work toward conquering nature and death? What makes countries come together in the United Nations to discuss an end to global conflict? Surely any student of history could teach world leaders that war has always been a part of the world, and always will be. It's endemic, and it can't be stopped. So why bother?

The answer is that we all believe deep in our hearts that these diseases can be conquered and that is why we agree that the money is well spent. The belief that human life can always progress on this planet and ultimately triumph over earth's imperfections is hard-wired into our brains. It is irrational and almost a matter of innate faith. We have no evidence that we will succeed at any of these endeavors. Nevertheless, it is practically ingrained in the human psyche that, against all the tangible evidence, we can make the world a better place, a concept that the Jewish people call *tikkun olam*, repair of the world.

Had you told people four hundred years ago that the average person would live to eighty-five or ninety years, they would have laughed out loud. In those days people had eight or nine children in the hope that two would reach maturity. One out of three women died in childbirth. Progress comes about specifically when we challenge the impossible, in the belief that man is the master of his environment. These achievements have come about because we have not accepted that nature is insurmountable.

Humankind's religious mandate is to push back the frontiers of nature and bring about, to the best of our ability, a perfect world purged of disease and inequity. Those who sit back and dismiss the world's imperfections as the will of God are guilty not only of misrepresenting God, but of failing in their own divine mission. God did not place us on this earth to be His apologists. He can do perfectly well without us, thank you very much. But those who are suffering desperately need us and our job is to be there for them.

We also have the right to demand that God correct the flaws of the world. It is entirely within His power to do so. Posturing to convince us suffering is necessary, or that we are responsible for all the bad things happening in this world, is demeaning to our intelligence and degrading to our sensibilities. We should not strive to make peace with human tragedy but to put an end to it. However abstract and difficult this concept may be to believe, we are capable of purging evil from the world through our united efforts, and demanding that God do the rest.

Thus, the real response to affliction is to create a world that welcomes in the final redemption. In this sense, Jews and Christians find common cause by both praying for the arrival of the Messiah and the fulfillment of the messianic prophecies foretold by the ancient Hebrew prophets, even if for the Jews it will be his first coming and for Christians it will be his second.

We can restore the true light and love of Judaism by demonstrating the power of our faith to inspire righteous action. While most Orthodox Jews live modest lives of exemplary honesty, hospitality, and communal devotion, too many engage in God apologetics. They are prone to the fraudulent belief that suffering is redemptive or is a punishment for sin. This has to be corrected.

Now is the time for the truths of our faith to shine ever more brightly. We must demonstrate that resting on the Sabbath and studying the Torah make individuals more noble, spiritual, and committed to helping those in distress. Our religion makes us defense attorneys for humanity, and prosecuting attorneys against those who cause innocents to suffer. We must teach our children not just the rituals that make them good Jews but the values that underpin these practices and foster their growth into intrinsically altruistic human beings.

Orthodox Judaism has reached its moment of truth. An increasing number of people no longer believe Jewish observance necessarily makes you a better person. Is there a correlation between observing the Sabbath and being honest in business? Is there a connection between wearing *tzitzit* and being faithful in marriage? When our daughters light the Sabbath candles, are we teaching them not only to continue the tradition of their matriarch Sarah but also to illuminate the earth's dark spaces? When our sons don yarmulkes, do they know that this is not only a symbol of our identity but also a call to action – to demonstrate love and compassion whenever they come upon any of God's children in despair?

Have we allowed ourselves at times to be religious without being spiritual, to be prayerful without being humble, to be ritually pedantic without being sensitive to the responsibilities of our partnership with God in this world? As part of their yeshivah education, our children should learn not only to say a blessing before eating an apple, but that the purpose of this blessing is to instill gratitude and a sense of connectedness between all living things as creations of the one God. And there is no more effective way to demonstrate that connectedness than to alleviate human suffering wherever it is found.

There should be no room in our communities for people who preach hatred or discrimination.

Let us destroy the myth held by our less observant Jewish brothers and sisters that Orthodox Jews are insular, judgmental, and indifferent to the suffering of those of a different community. Jewish insularity has no place among a people charged with being "a light unto the nations" (Isaiah 42:6, 49:6). Let us welcome all denominations into our homes, where they will see our daughters raised to comport themselves with dignity and to become scholarly, our sons craving the contents of books rather than the latest video games, and our resources utilized to do good deeds and host guests from near and far. In our various cities, we Orthodox rabbis must reach out to our Conservative and Reform colleagues in friendship and respect, even as we strictly maintain our Orthodox beliefs, to unify our commitment to ending injustice and elevating spiritual development within our congregations.

Many secular Jews look at observant men in long black coats and religious women wearing wigs and see something primitive, backward, even embarrassing. And when a handful of Orthodox people do something wrong these Jews rush to condemn the entire Orthodox community in an effort to disassociate themselves from a group they find unseemly. How sad that they are reinforced for being dismissive of their Jewish brothers and sisters, who live righteous lives distinguished by piety and eternal fidelity to the Jewish tradition. Isn't it time we accept that we are one people, whether we look like it or not, for the betterment of all? And what better way than to purge ourselves of the belief that Jewish suffering is the result of divine disfavor?

The Jewish people are, and have been, the most loyal, faithful, and devoted servants of God the world has ever seen. For millennia we have been prepared to be tortured and killed for our faithfulness to God's covenant. We deserve God's love rather than His judgment, His protection rather than the world's unprovoked attacks, and divine grace rather than human hate. It is in God's power to grant all these things and it is high time we demanded it.

At its core, *religion is the subordination of our self-centeredness to God's higher purpose*. It's the inspiration behind altruism and empathy. It teaches that *one good deed – even if it isn't captured on YouTube – has the power to change the world*. But it is rendered powerless when it becomes a superstition, with our own needs rather than God's will at its center.

So why isn't religion reversing the suffering inherent in our world? Perhaps it's because religion has been drafted into the service of contemporary society's insatiability. God has become yet another avenue for material gain. Pastors preach prosperity theology, where God is He Who provides a promotion at work. Rabbis watch in silence as their congregants turn spiritual celebrations into extravaganzas of superficial excess. Islamic usurpers of an otherwise great faith promise virgins and paradise to those who strike a murderous blow, subverting God's higher purpose for mankind by committing perversions in Allah's name.

Yet it is religion, not politics, that teaches that all humans are of equal and infinite value, with an importance far beyond ephemeral material objects. It is religion that teaches that family is sacred and marriage a sacrament, and that relationships are a more reliable road to happiness than career. We would all do well to heed the reminder of Moses, "Man does not live on bread

alone but on every word that comes from the mouth of the Lord"
(Deuteronomy 8:3), and recognize that *our faith holds a cure for
materialism and a formula for true growth and joy.*

# PART IV

# WHERE DO WE GO FROM HERE?

# CHAPTER 15

# WE ARE THE WORLD

---

Woe to those who call evil good and good evil, who put darkness for light and light for darkness, who put bitter for sweet and sweet for bitter. *(Isaiah 5:20)*

Trust in the Lord with all your heart and lean not on your own understanding... *(Proverbs 3:5–6)*

Even though I walk through the valley of the shadow of death I will fear no evil, for you are with me... *(Psalms 23:4)*

---

I would not say that a nation must be religious to be healthy. But it is clear that those nations that prosper have religious values, even if they are not themselves religious. A case in point is the State of Israel. Its majority population by far is secular, yet the nation is informed and influenced by the Jewish values upon which it is built.

I was in Israel when I received the terrible news that thirty of our bravest fellow Americans, twenty-two of them Navy Seals, were killed by a Taliban rocket in August 2011. While it was only one among many other headlines on the evening news in the US, in Israel such a tragedy would have sent the entire nation into paroxysms of national mourning. My great country of the United States could learn from the Israeli people about more greatly cherishing the life and memory of every soldier lost. Israel was founded on the Jewish value of treasuring and appreciating life, and when life is lost, especially lives committed to protecting the innocent, all grieve.

In Israel over recent years, wherever you traveled, you'd see signs demanding the freeing of Gilad Shalit, the Israeli soldier who was held for more than five years (June 2006–October 2011) like an animal in a cage by Hamas – a prime example of evil. "See, I set before you today life and prosperity, death and destruction," said Moses. "Now choose life, so that you and your children may live" (Deuteronomy 30:15, 19). These are the values that impelled Israel's highly controversial trade of a thousand terrorists to free Gilad and preserve his life.

Last year I took forty young Americans to visit Israel for the first time under the umbrella of the Birthright Israel program, which was founded by my dear friend Michael Steinhardt and is supported these days principally by the noted philanthropists Sheldon and Miriam Adelson. In Tel Aviv, we were guests of America's outstanding ambassador, Dan Shapiro, and heard a briefing on all that America does to support democracies like Israel. As we emerged onto the street, I spontaneously led our group in a proud rendition of Lee Greenwood's deeply moving song "God Bless the USA." It was a spontaneous hymn to our country, and its potential as a paragon of benevolence and kindness.

A few days later, when I was in Washington, DC, to speak at a conference, I took my kids to the Marine, Air Force, and World War II monuments, explaining that the US military is today the foremost force for good in the entire world, liberating the imprisoned, standing up for the oppressed, and lending women dignity and rights throughout the world. And it's no coincidence that its greatness is marked by service not to glory but to the defeat of evil, not to expand an empire but to crush tyranny, not to subdue a foreign nation but to stop the genocide of a defenseless people.

A global human recommitment to the infinite value of life, evidenced in particular by an abhorrence of human suffering and evil, is critical in this time when we are becoming inured to the daily deluge of horror stories in the media. As I surveyed the many tragedies that have filled the airways since the tenth anniversary of 9/11, I found I was slowly becoming desensitized to the murder of children and the immeasurable concurrent loss of human potential. From the freeing of Casey Anthony, who partied while her daughter decomposed in a Florida wood; to the dismembering of Leiby Kletsky, whose only sin was to inquire of Levi Aron how he might find his way home; the indiscriminate slaughter of seventy-six Norwegians, mostly young campers, by a nefarious villain; and the senseless drug-addled death of Amy Winehouse, I discovered that for all modern society's protestations of the infinite value of every person, human life is cheap and being further discounted by the day.

The death of Amy Winehouse was particularly indicative of that "thrift." Not because she was more famous than other victims or had more fans to grieve her loss, but because of all the deaths that made the news, hers might have been the most preventable. Perhaps we can't stop every neighborhood monster from chopping up children. I am hard-pressed to imagine what might have been done to forestall a summer campground in Norway from turning into a killing field. But we did know Amy Winehouse was drugging herself to oblivion and that terrible influences in her life were keeping her flying higher than the Hindenburg. We knew her lyrics, "*They tried to make me go to rehab, I said, No, no, no,*" were shockingly personal, and biographies of the singer listed so many public drug incidents that her body had become a walking pharmacy. Still, the paparazzi gathered. Still we amused ourselves with tabloid reports of her drunken concerts and slurred lyrics. Still we were regaled by media tales of her punching people in the face. Until, one day, she didn't wake up and it wasn't that entertaining anymore.

Michael Jackson was also a source of unending tabloid delight until his potion of Propofol closed his eyes forever. Was it the orphaning of his three children that touched us? Or the momentary loss of a reliable source of watercooler delight? What is it about our society that has so caricatured celebrities that their suffering awakens little human feeling, as if they were nothing more than cartoon characters that get squashed by a giant hammer only to pop right back up for our amusement? Was seeing the contorted faces of Janis and Mitch Winehouse at their daughter's funeral enough to remind us that Thor, Captain America, and Ironman are fictional characters while drugged, drunk, and dead celebrities are all too human and all too frail?

American popular culture is both adored and reviled the world over. People have screamed for Madonna from Tokyo to Santiago, for the Rolling Stones from Sydney to Singapore, for Michael Jackson from Bucharest to Kuala Lumpur. At the same time the world professes a revulsion for many things American. Protests against the building of MacDonald's and Starbucks franchises have been lodged from Motueka, New Zealand, to Beirut, Lebanon. Nowhere is this love-hate relationship more pronounced than in Europe. The Académie française regularly resists the "pollution" of the French language with American vocabulary. British politicians including former Labour MPs George Galloway and Ken Livingstone regularly characterize America as a warmongering, corrupt society.

One of the foremost examples cited by Europeans as to America becoming a country of knuckle-dragging Neanderthals is the fact that we still have the death penalty while Europe has abolished it utterly. I'm wondering, therefore, what my European friends are currently thinking about Anders Behring Breivik, who pleaded not guilty to the massacre in Norway of seventy-seven people, most of whom were teenagers. Breivik cited "self-defense" as the reason for his rampage seeing as he was trying to stop Norway from being overrun by Muslims (who were not among his victims). He added chillingly, "I would have done it again."

And here's the best part. Having been found to be mentally competent, Breivik was given the toughest sentence Norwegian law can mete out: twenty-one years. Although Norwegian law allows his sentence to be extended if he is found to still be a danger to society at the end of his term, Breivik could theoretically be walking the streets by the time he's fifty-five.

Counter to my European friends' claims that the death penalty is abhorrent, I would ask them whether they feel that seeing a man who killed seventy-seven people sipping a latte at a sidewalk café is not more so. My close friend Dennis Prager, the well-known author and radio host, once said that the death penalty, where it is truly warranted, is actually the more compassionate thing to do since the idea of a mass murderer being freed from prison inflicts a sadistic cruelty on the families of the murderer's victims.

To be sure, the Mishnah famously says that any court that put more than two people to death in a period of seventy years was considered murderous,[1] which demonstrates how absolutely meticulous and careful any court must be before it metes out the ultimate punishment. But surely Breivik, even according to this most compassionate of opinions, would be one of the two. If a mass murderer of approximately seventy young people merits

---

1   "The Sanhedrin who executes a person once in seven years is considered pernicious. Rabbi Eliezer ben Azariah said: Even one who does so once in seventy years is considered such" (Mishnah *Makkot* 1:10).

being freed from incarceration after just two decades, then justice has no meaning and the world we live in is utterly lawless.

In the United States we were horrified when a gunman with Joker-esque orange and red hair strolled into a Colorado movie theater in July 2012 and killed twelve people as they took in a Batman movie. Now think about Breivik's seventy-seven victims and imagine him walking the streets in his fifties, enjoying a cool morning breeze.

Europeans can mock us all they want, but one of the distinguishing characteristics of the United States of America is its hatred of evil and its constant preparedness to fight it. Whether it's our twenty-eight thousand troops currently protecting South Korea from the new North Korean thug Kim Jong-un or our brave service men and women fighting the wicked Taliban, America has always fought tyranny while the rest of the world has often preferred to hide their heads in the sand.

Mass murderers in cold blood are wicked beyond comprehension and do not deserve to walk God's green earth along with the righteous. If they are found guilty after a proper inquiry and absolutely fair trial, we must dispatch mass killers to the hell they deserve. Leaving them alive to one day walk free is deeply contemptuous of the many lives they have snuffed out and trivializes the unending grief of their surviving relatives.

Likewise, when our nation sees a tyrant and bully like Saddam Hussein who gasses children, we remove him from power, just as Britain and France courageously did to Muammar Gaddafi, with the help of American air power and following the lead of the brave Libyan people. Maybe even Europe admits it has something to learn from us backward Americans.

Fighting evil is not primitive nor Neanderthaloid but is rather deeply moral and demonstrates a commitment to the infinite value of every human life.

People the world over need to recommit to this value, which so often gets lost in the maelstrom of our materialistic, technology-driven lives today. My conclusion that we are all becoming desensitized to the value of life, especially children's lives, was readily captured by the bizarre criticism of the one tabloid story that should have brought us a little cheer. Instead, the announcement that David and Victoria Beckham had just given birth to a fourth child brought derision in many British circles for the couple having too many children and overpopulating the earth, a sad attitude that parents of large families often encounter.

For the record, my wife and I, thank God, have nine children. Every child brings great blessings in his or her wake. With my children I have RV'd all around North America. I have taken them to countless lectures, debates, museums, and of course, synagogues. At our weekly Friday night Shabbat dinner table, we host people from every culture, religion, and nationality, and we are blessed with giggles and conversations. The more children we have had, the more joy has come into our lives. And yes, parents with large families have active and fulfilling sex lives, as I discovered from interviewing hundreds of them for my books *Kosher Sex*, *Kosher Adultery*, and the *Kosher Sutra*. Where do we find the time for everything? With a large family you learn to economize both resources and time. Your heart expands and you develop healthier priorities. The older children help with the younger children, and the family becomes a lovingly fueled and endlessly resourceful unit.

In the summer of 2008, the *New York Times* magazine published a cover story entitled "Disappearing Europe" that explained countries like France, Norway, and Russia had hit "lowest low fertility," having so few babies they cannot replenish their numbers even in two generations. In the 1960s, as the *New York Times* notes, Europe constituted 20 percent of the world's population. Today, the number has fallen to under 10 percent, despite massive efforts to boost birth rates. How ironic that as the West has become richer and more capable of affording children it has lost its appetite for kids. Does real happiness stem instead from a BMW or a Prada handbag?

From parents who ignore their kids as they work long hours to keep up with the Joneses, to spiritual rites of passage like weddings and bar mitzvahs becoming more about impressing friends than celebrating family milestones and acknowledging God's presence, money and fame have become an obsession. Once, a couple came to me for counseling because the wife wanted a second child while her husband complained they couldn't afford it. When the session was over I was dumbstruck as they drove away in their brand new Porsche. There is a shocking failure of religion to instill values in a culture that so desperately needs to be reminded of what is truly important.

And we cannot, of course, overlook the fact that many ostensibly "religious" people are guilty of the very horrors we rail against – from the Hamas-fired missile directed at an Israeli school bus to Christian fanatics like Scott Roeder who murder abortion doctors[2] and the Jewish mass murderer Baruch Goldstein, who perpetrated the Cave of the Patriarchs massacre.[3] The authority of religion is compromised by the evil perpetrated by those who claim active membership in its fold when the leaders of that religion do not condemn the murderous actions taken in the name of faith. Imams, rabbis, priests, and pastors have an unending

---

2   On May 31, 2009, Roeder, who identified with the Christian anti-abortion terrorist group Army of God, walked into a Wichita, Kansas, church and shot to death the abortion provider Dr. George Tiller, who was at that moment serving as an usher during prayer services.

3   On February 25, 1994, Goldstein opened fire on unarmed Muslim worshippers in the Cave of the Patriarchs in Hebron, Israel, killing 29 and injuring another 125 before he was himself killed.

responsibility to condemn all violence perpetrated in the name of religion, as well as launch initiatives dedicated to eradicating suffering wherever it has gained a foothold. Islam especially runs the risk in our time of compromising its deep moral message with a tsunami of killers who believe they are striking a blow for the faith when they dismember pregnant women with bombs. They must be strongly condemned by peace-loving imams throughout the world, failing which a great world religion will be overrun by murderers who fire katyushas while yelling "Allahu Akbar."

America has a bedrock of religious values that underpins its moral clarity. We mustn't allow these values to get lost. We must honor every life. We must cherish our children. We must punish those who destroy life.

I protest the tendency to immediately declare those guilty of a heinous crime "insane." In a televised debate on the *Joy Behar Show* between me and Father Edward Beck, the prominent Catholic cleric – with whom I am friendly and whom I deeply respect – still excused Caylee Anthony's partying in nightclubs after the death of her daughter by claiming she had probably snapped. He found Levi Aron equally not responsible for his actions, though Aron told police he understood what he did "may be wrong," was "sorry for the hurt he caused," and demonstrated an ability to distinguish between righteous and immoral behavior. Anders Breivik's attorney claimed his client was crazy even as Anders argued his actions were a European declaration of war against Islam. In the end the court found him sane (and guilty), and when he was asked whether he intended to appeal the verdict, Breivik asserted that he did not recognize the legitimacy of the court and that he "would like to apologise to all militant nationalists in Norway and in Europe for not having killed more people."[4]

---

4   "Survivors Hope Breivik Verdict Ends Year of 'Hell,'" *ABC News*, August 25, 2012.

Is it not possible that each of these individuals was evil rather than insane? Are we, as a culture, simply afraid to distinguish between the two? Remember that I started this book with someone challenging me on my own reluctance to use the word *evil*.

It's up to us; the choice is ours: **What are we going to stand for?**

# CHAPTER 16

# WHAT DOES GOD WANT?

---

Whoever shuts their ears to the cry of the poor will also cry out and not be answered. *(Proverbs 21:13)*

Should not a people inquire of their God? *(Isaiah 8:19)*

Lord, you have seen this; do not be silent. Do not be far from me, Lord. Awake, and rise to my defense! Contend for me, my God and Lord. *(Psalms 35:22–23)*

---

The patriarch Jacob is the most maligned of all the patriarchs. With his seeming deception of his blind father to gain the firstborn blessing from Esau and his commercial manipulations of his father-in-law Laban, most of whose flock he eventually owned, he is treated by anti-Semites as the prototype of the wily, cunning, dishonest Jew who will do anything for profit. Jacob is the forerunner of Shylock, who mourns more for his lost ducats than his lost daughter Jessica. He is the father, they say, of the modern State of Israel that will engage in questionable moral tactics to fight off its enemies.

And yet, the Jews celebrate Jacob and call themselves his, rather than Abraham's, offspring. We are the children of Israel, the name given to Jacob after he wrestled with, and defeated, an angel.

Why celebrate a man of seeming deceit?

Because Jacob was the first patriarch who decided he would enter into the arena with evil, fight it, and defeat it. The damage this would do to his reputation did not concern him. He knew Esau was violent and dangerous and would have abused the power that would have come with the firstborn blessing. He was determined to stop him one way or another. The same was true of Laban, a cunning man not above selling his daughters in return for free labor, robbing others to achieve wealth, and swindling Jacob out of fourteen years of unpaid labor.

There are those who believe that religion should distance itself from the corruption of the world and maintain an unblemished integrity. Monastic life, divorced from the affairs of a society ruled by greed and avarice, is where the pious flourish. Even in the Jewish world there are many who believe that the righteous man spends his life studying, unsullied by materialism or commerce.

To some degree this was the posture adopted by Abraham, who was known as Ha'ivri, the Hebrew, the man who sets himself apart. The kernel of monotheism, having just been birthed by Abraham, was, he felt, too vulnerable to be exposed to the world's malevolent influence. So he cloistered himself from immoral people like Sodom and Gomorrah's inhabitants. Yes, he would pray for their welfare from afar, but he would not live among them, attempt to influence them, or even combat their wickedness. Isaac, who was a holy offering brought on God's altar, likewise lives apart and is prohibited by God from sojourning in the fleshpots of Egypt.

Only Jacob engages the world and courageously confronts the wicked, allowing goodness to triumph. Yes, at times he will fight them on their own terms – even employ their own means – to defeat them. But he will not let the world be ruled by wicked men. One way or another, he will stop them. And it is as a result of this courageous posture to fight God's battles that his name is changed from Jacob – he who is stepped on by the heel – to Israel, he who wrestles with God and man and triumphs. In the act of this constant struggle against malevolent forces who seek to defeat him, Jacob gives birth to a new concept of religion whose theme is captured by that name. Not the subservient man of the spirit, but the rebellious man of faith.

Indeed, it is those who are prepared to fight evil even when accused of becoming unethical in the process that are vindicated by history as having saved civilization from monstrous injustice. Lincoln suspended habeus corpus, insisted on continuing the bloody engagements of the civil war when there was an outcry for peace, and was labeled a bloodthirsty tyrant for doing so. Today, we remember him as our greatest president, who purged America of the abomination of slavery and kept the Union intact. Had he not hated the evil of slavery, would we today consider him a great man? While Chamberlain waved his useless piece of paper proclaiming "peace in our time" and portrayed himself as an ethical man unwilling to shed blood, Churchill was dismissed as a warmonger and alarmist provoking a fight with Hitler. He would later be accused of mass butchery in leveling cities like Hamburg and Dresden to finish off the Third Reich. Yet, today he is remembered as the twentieth century's greatest statesman.

When I was in Oxford I heard world-renowned Jewish academics lamenting the State of Israel's existence. Prior to its creation, they maintained, the Jews had the respect of the world as the people of the book and the pity of humanity as Hitler's victims. Now we were the people of the M-16 assault rifle and seen as oppressors of the Palestinians. Yet these moral cowards would have Hezbollah, Hamas, and Iran take over the Middle East in order for the Jews to maintain a false morality, predicated on ethical self-preservation, while the world is overtaken by darkness. The desire to remain aloof from the world's affairs and allow wicked men to gain supremacy is the piety of cowards and betrays a fraudulent faith.

Rather, the quintessential man of faith was he who demanded of God Himself to keep his promises and His injunctions to choose life. After Moses was sent to free the Israelite slaves of Egypt, and Pharaoh responded coldly that their suffering would increase through the withholding of straw, Moses did not return to God with head bowed low, accepting the brutality inflicted on his people as God's will. "Why, Lord, why have you brought trouble on this people?" he says to the Creator of the Universe. "Ever since I went to Pharaoh to speak in your name, he has brought trouble on this people, and you have not rescued your people at all" (Exodus 5:22–23). The rebellious man of faith will continue to worship God after Auschwitz, but He will never excuse God's seeming callousness in allowing a holocaust against innocents.

The faithful have been obedient long enough. It is time for the emergence of the new defiant man of faith, steeped in the tradition of Jacob, refusing to allow the iron hoofs of evil to tread upon the vulnerable flesh of the innocent and the soft and trusting heart of the righteous.

Indeed, to be forbidden from testing God assures a hollow relationship with Him, an empty lie in which humanity does little more than bow its head in pathetic submission. Is that really what God wants? A congregation of sycophants? Was it not God Who commanded us to uphold life and to abhor death? Did the same God that commanded us to always oppose death and choose life ("For I take no pleasure in the death of anyone, declares the Sovereign Lord; repent and live" [Ezekiel 18:32]) suddenly want us to justify death, rationalize suffering, and accept calamity?

God wants us to do all we can to alleviate human suffering and to fulfill our instinct for survival. And when there is no more that we can do, He wants us to shake our fists at the heavens and demand that the Creator stop all human torment. God expects us, enjoins us, *commands* us, to challenge Him. That's what Jews have been praying for, for thousands of years: an end to death, material abundance, and the onset of a perfect world in the messianic epoch.

We have to do all in our power to resist the urge to vindicate God and implicate man when it comes to human suffering. We're always searching, probing, finessing any way to let God off the hook when it comes to human tragedy. I see it all around me. It's become a religious pandemic.

Arriving in LA to serve as scholar-in-residence one weekend, I picked up a handsome brochure on the weekly Torah reading. Contained therein was a short piece by a rabbi addressing the question of why some children are born with mental disability. The rabbi's answer, however well-intentioned, disturbed me deeply and I felt there had to be a response, lest unsuspecting readers conclude that always finding the hidden blessing in suffering is somehow an authentic religious response.

His argument, in a nutshell, was that souls come into this world and are confronted with moral choices. If they choose wrong it will tarnish them. It's a necessary risk that God is willing to take. But some souls are so lofty that God doesn't want to take any chances with them. So he puts them in a body, or empowers them with a mind, that will make it impossible for them to sin, thereby guaranteeing their innocence. The rest of us ought to just be awed by how special these souls are and inspired by the dedication of the people who love them, who teach us what true love is all about.

The shallow and unfortunate argument that mental disability is some sort of blessing goes against the grain of traditional Jewish thought. Simply stated, we are in the business of protesting to God against all human suffering. We never justify it. The word *Israel* translates as "he who wrestles with God." Whenever Jews witness human suffering, we never accept it, we do not seek to understand it, and we do not explain it away as something lofty and blessed. Indeed, one of the principal differences between Christianity and Judaism is that the former insists that suffering can be redemptive – as when Jesus suffers on the cross to pardon human sin – while the latter insists that suffering is a tragedy without redemptive merit that must be remedied and removed.

When Abraham is informed by God that he will destroy Sodom and Gomorrah for their sin, refusing to accept any virtue in the suffering of even the sinful, Abraham protests to God, "Will not the Judge of all the earth do right?" (Genesis 18:25). When God sends Moses to free the Jews from Egypt, but Pharaoh refuses and instead increases their workload, Moses offers this unbelievable protest: "Why, Lord, why have you brought trouble on this people? Is this why you sent me? Ever since I went to Pharaoh to speak in your name, he has brought trouble on this people, and you have not rescued your people at all" (Exodus 5:22–23). And then, most famously, after God threatens to annihilate the Jews after the sin of the golden calf, Moses says to God that if he carries out this threat and rains such devastation and suffering upon the people, "then blot me out of the book you have written" (Exodus 32:32). (I will expand on each of these shortly).

We Jews protest and remonstrate against suffering. We don't excuse it. We don't justify it. We don't find beauty in it. We don't find spiritual purpose it in. We fight it and, to the best of our ability, cure it.

I have no idea why God would allow any child to come into this world with severe mental or physical disability. What I do know, however, is that He shouldn't. Children deserve to be born with all their faculties and with all their abilities. All children deserve to be healthy. Those who come into the world with mental handicaps are, of course, beautiful children, the equal of every healthy child, deserving of infinite love, equality, and rights. They do indeed inspire us with their innocence. Indeed, given their special needs they require more of our love, more of our attention. What they do not deserve, however, and what they certainly have never earned, is our contemptuous effort to justify their suffering and their challenges by ascribing to them some unknown and lofty divine purpose.

To be sure, children with special needs most often have bright, luminous souls. They are indeed the very epitome of incorruptibility. Yet even as we love and cherish every Down syndrome child, we dare never dignify Down syndrome itself, and I honor all doctors who work tirelessly so that this disease can be purged and all children come into the world completely healthy.

In about 2001 a friend asked me if he could bring his thirty-something-year-old Down syndrome brother to meet the singer Michael Jackson. The young man loved Michael's music and did his own version of the moonwalk. I was Michael's rabbi and I asked him. He graciously agreed, and the young man, who was supposed to spend only about ten minutes with Michael, was there for much longer. Michael loved meeting him, and the attention the superstar gave the young man greatly endeared Michael to me. When he left, I asked Michael why he had given him so much time. "I'm jealous of him, Shmuley." Michael told me. "That man will always be a child, always be innocent. I'm envious."

Children with special needs have very special qualities. We will give them all the love and attention they require. But let us not make light of the challenges both they and their families endure. Divorce rates for parents of children with autism have been quoted as being as high as 80–90 percent, and while some debunk these numbers there can be no question that it puts an added strain on a relationship. Of course the effort is worth it, as every child is equal and of infinite value. It does mean, however, that offering these parents fraudulent comfort by inventing silly theological justifications for their children's challenges is not something that any religion should be in the business of.

So what should a rabbi or priest say to a parent who asks them why their child was born with severe disability? They should acknowledge their limitations and tell them the truth: "I don't know. I honestly have no idea. Why God does things is not our business. What we do know is that your child needs no spiritual reason to be here. He is beautiful, he is innocent, and he is exceptional. And you are not alone. You have a community. We are here with you. Your child is our child. Your baby is our baby. You will never have to raise your child alone and you will never be abandoned. God has a lot of explaining to do, but we have a lot of work to do. So rather than wasting time endeavoring to understand why this is, let's give your child the best programs and care so that he can have the most normal life possible."

A quick story is in order. Friends of mine had a baby with severe Down syndrome. The doctors told them the baby would need extensive surgery just to survive. They could forego the surgery and the baby would not live. Sobbing uncontrollably, the wife told her husband that she was not sure she was up to the task of raising the boy. It would take too much out of her, ruin their finances and possibly their marriage. The husband said, "We'll find the strength. This is our child." A month of intensive care and surgery commenced, and the baby survived. Today he is about fifteen years old. He needs tons of extra love and care, which his devoted parents and siblings provide. The family is immensely protective of him and they all take turns playing with him and even, at times, feeding him. They tell me he has taught them to love that much more deeply and that they would not give him up for the world. Even as I write this, I'm getting emotional because the circumstances are very moving. I have no idea why the child came into the world suffering. But I do know that his life is infinitely more precious than any explanation, and that any attempt to explain this life would never do justice to the grandeur of the boy's existence.

***Why does God allow the innocent to suffer? I have no idea. He shouldn't.*** But our job is to fill in the empty spaces God seemingly vacates in His universe and to act in God's stead, being as human and loving as we can. But equally, our role is to challenge God in the face of this suffering and demand – not request but demand – that it end.

# CHAPTER 17

# A TIME TO BE SILENT AND A TIME TO SPEAK

---

"Justice, justice shall you pursue" *(Deuteronomy 16:20)*

"Like a muddied spring or a polluted well are the righteous who give way to the wicked." *(Proverbs 25:26)*

"Then a great and powerful wind tore the mountains apart and shattered the rocks before the Lord, but the Lord was not in the wind. After the wind there was an earthquake, but the Lord was not in the earthquake. After the earthquake came a fire, but the Lord was not in the fire. And after the fire came a gentle whisper." *(I Kings 19:11–12)*

---

In one of my first weeks at the helm of the Chabad House in Oxford and the Oxford University L'Chaim Society, I was having the traditional Shabbat dinner with a group of students from the university when the subject of the Holocaust came up. I stated my position on the subject, much to the amazement and disappointment of some of the Orthodox students sitting at the table. I said that I cannot understand why God allowed the murder of six million Jews, nor will I accept it. I vociferously object – and I encouraged them as students to object – to the catastrophe that had been visited on our people. I said that any attempt to justify the Holocaust from a Jewish perspective was grossly immoral.

A heated debate ensued. In the midst of the discussion, three Orthodox students got up to leave. Clearly indignant, they asked me how I could question God's judgment and His ways. How could I refuse to accept God's deeds? They said they could not tolerate blasphemy in any form, let alone from an Orthodox rabbi.

"Blasphemy?" I responded. "If questioning God in response to other people's calamities and misfortunes constitutes blasphemy, then Abraham, Moses, the prophet Jeremiah, and the ministering angels in heaven were all blasphemers as well!"

They sat down again. I began to explain.

Where do we get the idea of objecting, of challenging God's justice, when confronted by other people's suffering? What makes this the authentic Jewish response to tragedy? It began with the first Jew, Abraham.

The book of Genesis relates very clearly how God came to Abraham before he destroyed the cities of Sodom and Gomorrah. God said, "Then the Lord said, "Shall I hide from Abraham what I am about to do? Abraham will surely become a great and powerful nation, and all nations on earth will be blessed through him" (Genesis 18:17–18).

So God discloses to Abraham his intention to destroy Sodom and all of its inhabitants. "The outcry against Sodom and Gomorrah is so great and their sin so grievous" (Genesis 18:20). Not only have they sinned but their immoral lifestyle poses a threat to all of the surrounding cities. Hence, they must suffer and be obliterated, lest they serve to influence the outlying areas in their immoral ways.

Now, how does Abraham react? The most upright and moral human being on earth, the man who abandoned idolatry and introduced to the world the concept of monotheism has just been told that on a hill not far from where he dwells is an evil inhabitance. This evil inhabitance threatens to undermine everything Abraham has accomplished in terms of elevating the world, promoting monotheism, and bringing people closer to God. This city is a bad influence on his child (and future children). It is just plain evil. Its inhabitants are corrupt and base. So God is going to put an end to this cancer. Does Abraham see this as a victory for himself? Does he say, *Blessed be God Who is destroying the wicked. O, God, please vanquish, punish, and annihilate those who oppose Your ways?*

No. He has the audacity to argue with God. He asks, *How could You, how could You?* "Far be it from you to do such a thing – to kill the righteous with the wicked, treating the righteous and the wicked alike. Far be it from you! Will not the Judge of all the earth do right?" (Genesis 18:25). And so he stood and sparred with God, pleading with Him to spare the city's inhabitants.

The question on this episode is this: There are people who do not believe that when the city is destroyed, God is behind it. Thus, they call it a bad thing. Maybe it's random, maybe it's a product of some evil force at work, but it is still evil. But Abraham certainly knew that God was behind the destruction of Sodom. God himself told Abraham, *I am going to do it. It is not a freak accident, I am doing it. I've thought it over. I have my reasons and I am going to destroy the city.* But in spite of this Abraham asks, *How could You?*

Now, where was Abraham's faith? In truth, he did not even require faith in this particular circumstance. God spoke to him directly and told him that He was going to punish Sodom. Shouldn't Abraham have thought that God is just and knows what He's doing? Wouldn't this have been a greater virtue than to challenge God? And how could the Torah, in telling us about the prototype for the Jewish people, the ideal Jew, how he served

God and how we must learn from his example, disclose to us that Abraham did not trust God's judgment?

What is even more puzzling is that later in the Torah when God comes to Abraham and tells him, "Take your son, your only son, whom you love – Isaac – and go to the region of Moriah. Sacrifice him there as a burnt offering on a mountain I will show you" (Genesis 22:2), Abraham offers no resistance whatsoever. God has just told him that he must put his own son, a young innocent man, to death, and how does Abraham react? "Early the next morning Abraham got up and loaded his donkey" (Genesis 22:3). Not only does he execute the command, he does so enthusiastically. He gets up early! He performs God's request with zest and humility. But what happened to justice? Why not object to the command to end the life of your only son? Abraham can object to the destruction of Sodom but not to that of his own son?

What we can extract from this episode is: God is in control of everything, and just as the Berdichever (a Hasidic rabbi) says, as long as it is You, O God, Who is in control of what is happening, then the event must be good. But all of this only applies if some misfortune is befalling oneself. Thus, when God tells Abraham that he has a tragedy coming his way in the form of the death of his son, Abraham submits and accepts it. But if it is happening to someone else our reaction must be that although we believe that God is good, and although we know that God is causing this misfortune and that God certainly has His reasons, nevertheless we are commanded by God to pursue justice. And justice cannot be pursued on a level of faith.

God commands man in the most emphatic of terms: "Justice, justice shall you pursue" (Deuteronomy 16:20). In order to have justice, one must have proof. Thus, for a human being, who is not all knowing, to accept that something dreadful is happening in Sodom and not be bothered by it because he has faith in God is an insufficient and flawed response. As far as faith, his faith is perfect, but where is his pursuit of justice and righteousness? God may have his reasons and thus for God it is just to afflict Sodom. But where is this person's justice? Where is his evidence that the people of Sodom are deserving of this punishment and that what is happening is just and good?

God's commandment to man is to establish justice, and always to promote life, not to trust that God is just. The question of God's justice is a non sequitur. Of course He is just. But this is not the issue. The real question is this: Are *we* just? Where is our concern for another human being? God created us with a mind and a heart and told us to pursue justice until we actually achieve justice. When it comes to issues of life and death God wishes for us to affirm life and challenge those who would deny it. God is the judge of the earth. He requires no helpers. But He does expect us to concern ourselves only with an affirmation of life.

Thus, immediately at the beginning of our history, it was established that everything that transpires is by divine plan. God is behind it. There are no two Gods. We believe that God is fully in control. But even as we retain the faith that God knows what He is doing, we object to what we cannot see.

Here, in effect, we come across the idea of dual roles or purposes. There are times when equally valid and appropriate roles actually conflict without invalidating each other. Rather, each party has a different role to play. For instance, in the parent-child relationship, it is the duty of the child to remain a child, and it is the duty of the parent to discipline the child and try to get him to behave better. So the parent runs around correcting the child, getting angry at him for making a mess or writing on the walls. But if the child were to stop behaving as a child, if he were to suddenly just sit around doing nothing and act like an adult, the parent would become terribly worried. She would take him to the doctor and ask him what is wrong with her child. And what parent would be happy with a child who behaves like an adult at the age of seven? So although her role of disciplining the child and his role of running amok and being naughty conflict, both are not only acceptable, but proper.

In effect God says to us, *I am the Creator of the universe and I have a job to do. I give life and I take life. I give health and I deny health. I am the Master of the world and there will be times when I will be taking life. I may take somebody's happiness or their health. And when I do any of these things, I don't need your help. Don't doubt that I am doing it, and don't doubt that I know what I'm doing and that what I'm doing is just. But stay out of these deliberations. They are My domain.*

*On the other hand, when I give life,* God says, *when I distribute health and happiness, here I invite you to join me. Assist me in bestowing goodness.* This is the correct definition of good and evil. A bad thing is anything we do in which God forbade our participation. God said that He is in control of death; we dare not assist him. On the other hand, a good thing is anything we do in which God enjoins us to participate. So doing a *mitzvah* like giving charity and enhancing another's life is good. But stealing and detracting from someone else's livelihood or causing our fellow human sorrow, grief, or pain is a sin.

Moses is told by God on the occasion of the Jews building a golden calf in the desert, "I have seen these people," the Lord said to Moses, "and they are a stiff-necked people. Now leave me alone so that my anger may burn against them and that I may destroy them. Then I will make you into a great nation" (Exodus 32:9–10). Does Moses comply? God Himself has told him that the Jews deserve destruction, and He has even told Moses to refrain from defending them and objecting to God's intention. But what does Moses do?

Here I must get personal. Every year when this portion of the Bible is read in Sabbath services in the synagogue, I get goose bumps, for the ensuing words of Moses constitute the single most eloquent defense of human life recorded in the Bible. Moses stands his ground. He is not prepared to let the Jews die without a fight. He stands tall and argues with his Creator. His mission is to save the Jews, and at this he will not fail. "But Moses sought the favor of the Lord his God. 'Lord,' he said, 'why should your anger burn against your people, whom you brought out of Egypt with great power and a mighty hand? ...Turn from your fierce anger; relent and do not bring disaster on your people'" (Exodus 32:11–12).

Subsequently, Moses uses even stronger tactics to elicit a pardon from God on behalf of the Jewish people. "So Moses went back to the Lord and said, 'Oh, what a great sin these people have committed! They have made themselves gods of gold. But now, please forgive their sin – but if not, then blot me out of the book you have written'" (Exodus 32:31–32). Where in the history of religion do we ever have a human who asks the Almighty to be purged from His holy book because he wishes to be disassociated from a God Who is not forgiving and loving?

What kind of audacity does it take on the part of a mortal being to blackmail God? How could Moses object to God's judgment when God comes to him and warns him, "Do not try to stop me" from destroying the Jews? How could Moses rebel against God?

The answer to this critical question is in the directive itself. The Talmud (*Berakhot* 32) notes that God tells Moses "Do not try to stop me" (or alternatively translated: "Leave me alone") before Moses even opened his mouth in defense of the Jewish people. In the words of Rashi, "We have not yet heard that Moses prayed for them, yet God says, 'Let me alone.' However, here He opened a door for Moses and informed him that the matter depended upon him, that if he will pray for them, He will not exterminate them." In other words, what God was saying to Moses was this: *My responsibility is to punish and cleanse those who are deserving. But you, Moses, why are you just sitting there listening to all of this? Why haven't you opened your mouth to protest My planned destruction of the Jewish people? As a human being you have an entirely different responsibility from Mine. You must affirm life, not blindly accept My judgment. The Jews need an advocate. Plead for them.*

The idea of responding to suffering in the form of protest and challenging God's judgment is found again in the Talmud in relation to Moses. Commenting on Moses' request of God, "I beseech You to show Me your glory," the Talmud explains that what Moses was asking was, "Why are there righteous people who suffer?" Likewise at the destruction of the first Temple, the prophet Jeremiah asks God, "Why do the wicked prosper?" (*Berakhot* 7a).

King David the psalmist implicates God in the face of human suffering: "Awake, Lord! Why do you sleep? Rouse yourself! Do not reject us forever. Why do you hide your face and forget our misery and oppression? We are brought down to the dust; our bodies cling to the ground. Rise up and help us; rescue us because of your unfailing love" (Psalms 44:23–26).

The prophet Isaiah complains to God in the same vein: "Our holy and glorious temple, where our ancestors praised you, has been burned with fire, and all that we treasured lies in ruins. After all this, Lord, will you hold yourself back? Will you keep silent and punish us beyond measure?" (Isaiah 64:11–12). The prophet Habakkuk adds his voice to the chorus: "How long, Lord, must I call for help, but you do not listen? Or cry out to you, 'Violence!' but you do not save?" (Habakkuk 1:2).

Even among the ministering angels there is a tradition of challenging God in the face of human suffering. One of the most famous examples of this is to be found in our Yom Kippur prayer books in the story of the Ten Saintly Martyrs who were put to death by the Roman emperor. After the horrific murder of Rabbi Yishmael the high priest, in which the skin of his face was flayed off, we read, "The heavenly angels cried out in bitter grief: Is this the Torah and such its reward! O You Who enwrap Yourself with light as with a garment, the foe blasphemes Your great and awesome name, scorns and desecrates the words of the Torah."

Therefore, a person may not point a gun at an innocent person and think to himself, "Since God is the master of the universe and nothing transpires outside His will, therefore if my intended victim dies after I pull the trigger, it will be God's will. So there is nothing wrong with me shooting at him." This kind of thinking is wrong. But it is wrong not because one might kill a person who was *not* meant to die, but rather, as Rabbi Manis Friedman says, because one might kill a person who *is* meant to die – and that is a sin. Death is totally in God's domain. It is His affair and not ours. Our business is life.

Can one imagine a patient being brought before a religious, God-fearing doctor and the doctor refusing to treat him, saying, *Let God decide. First, if God wants this person to be sick, then who am I to question God's judgment or reverse His will? Obviously, this person must be a sinner and is receiving his just reward. Second, if God wishes the patient to die, then at the end of the day all of my efforts will be in vain. And if He does not wish him to die, then my efforts are not even needed. Therefore I refuse to treat him.* This doctor is not only a crackpot, but is grossly immoral and acts in contradiction to God's will. If someone is sick and there is a possibility of healing him, we are commanded by God to *run* to heal him, not to engage in theological polemics.

And if one is to ask, "Who are we to interfere with God's plan?" in this half of God's plan we are not only invited, but obligated, to interfere. We must offer a cure. The duty and obligation for doctors to heal is a godly obligation, not just a concession. And our responsibility as humans is not to focus on the success of our efforts. Even if it appears that a patient has little or no hope of living, we must still endeavor to save each person, for God never told us to be successful at saving lives, but rather *to concern ourselves* with the saving of life.

Interestingly, the Torah instructs man, "Do not stand by when your friend's blood is being shed" (Leviticus 19:16). But the literal translation is "Do not stand on his blood," as if the blood has already been shed. What this is telling us is, Rabbi Friedman added, is that it is very possible that one may come across a person whose blood has already been shed, a person who is destined to die for some divine cosmic reason. His blood is already shed, theoretically. Yet even then we have a commandment of not standing on his blood. We cannot be passive and allow him to die even when his death is preordained. One must object to this individual's death even though one is a believer and accepts that no one dies before his time. One must object as did our forefather Abraham. Indeed God knows what He is doing, but until we see an intelligible reason for why this individual is dying, we must try to prevent it from happening. One must attempt to heal, pray, and plead on his behalf.

*Challenging God for the pain He causes human beings is not a contradiction to faith. Rather, it enforces the belief that everything emanates from and is dependent on God.* It is much like the obligation to pray, whose central premise, according to Maimonides, is that man acknowledges his total dependence on God. Maimonides maintains that the obligation to pray to God arises every time man is in need of physical sustenance. In this way man comes to recognize that it is God Who controls his world, and it is to Him that man must pay homage. In the same way, challenging and asking God to rescind the suffering caused to humans acknowledges that all things come from God, the good and the bad, and it is to Him and to Him only that supplications must be offered.

The story is told that in the Baal Shem Tov's early years, the great Hasidic master would devote almost all of his time to traveling around the Russian countryside asking unlearned Jewish peasants how they were doing. They would respond, "*Baruch Hashem* (thank God) – however we are, we thank God." Eliciting this response from the simple Jewish country folk was the Baal Shem Tov's purpose from the beginning. He would travel all over Russia just to get a simple Jew to say "*Baruch Hashem.*" And why all the effort? "Because," the Baal Shem Tov explained, "God has no greater pleasure than hearing the heartfelt, sincere, and straightforward proclamation of faith on the part of a simple, yet devout and pious Jew." The statement of "thank God" – the acknowledgment on the part of the individual that for good or for bad, it is God Who controls the world – these are the things that God wishes to hear most.

In effect, when we do challenge God and demand that He rescind his decrees, we are not introducing any new concepts of justice and forcing God to conform to our standards of morality and fairness. Rather, what we are saying to Him is this: It was You Who told us about the obligation to "love your fellow as yourself." And it was You Who taught us to be sensitive to the suffering of all our fellow creatures, including animals, as in the commandment that before one removes the eggs from a nest, one must first send away the mother bird so as not to grieve her. And it was You Who taught us always to feel the pain of an orphan and a widow, as well as to make a convert feel at home. And it was You Who taught us not to stand idly by the sick but to engage in medical practice so as to heal them. And it was You Who obligated us to always be generously responsive to the poor and destitute. *Should You, then, not do the same?*

Was it not You Who described yourself, at Your very essence, as being "the compassionate and gracious God, slow to anger, abounding in love and faithfulness, maintaining love to thousands, and forgiving wickedness, rebellion and sin" (Exodus 34:6–7). Was it not You Who described Yourself as the One Who listens to the poor workman who has given away his only cloak as security for a loan? Should You then not listen to our pleas for this poor soul who languishes in pain and misery? In other words, we are obliging God to keep to the standards and practices that He Himself instituted as special and sacred.

What was Abraham's attitude to God after the city of Sodom had been destroyed? He had begged, pleaded, and bargained on their behalf. Was Abraham's faith shaken by what had happened? Certainly not. His response was to hang his head in acceptance: "*Baruch Dayan Emet*" (Blessed is the True Judge). This response, which has traditionally been recited by Jews upon hearing evil tidings, acknowledges that ultimately it is only God Who knows what is right and what is wrong.

But if this was Abraham's response after the event, why did he not spare himself the effort of arguing in the first place? Instead of challenging God's justice and then, after the event, affirming his belief in divine justice, why not just say *Baruch Dayan Emet* when he first heard of God's plans to punish the guilty and forget about the whole affair? If indeed Abraham had that much faith in God's goodness, then why did he save it for the end?

It has to do with obligations, as we mentioned earlier. We challenge God's intention because this is what God requires of us. God wants us to affirm life. And so long as there is any possibility of enhancing life and alleviating suffering, we are obligated to do whatever is in our ability to achieve those ends. If there is a possibility that this person can be saved, that this person can be healed, that this person can be cured, that this situation can be salvaged, then we must save whatever can be saved.

And what if God's answer to our prayers is no? Reb Aryeh Levin, who was warmly known by everyone as the Saint of

Jerusalem, was once posed this question by a woman who had prayed with all her might and shed impassioned tears for her sick husband, who died nonetheless. Reb Aryeh replied to her that every single one of those tears are stored in heaven, and when evil decrees or calamities are looming over the world, each of these prayers and tears serves as a shield to protect from these events. If those prayers did not heal her husband, somewhere else in the world, some other good person is benefiting from her entreaties to the Almighty. While this is in no way an answer for why this tragedy struck this woman, it still gives us strength to know that our prayers are never wasted.

And it helps console us, for after the fact, once we see that nothing more can be done, we must accept God's ultimate judgment, fairness, and wisdom and recite *Baruch Dayan Emet*. Once things are over and done with, we are no longer obligated to try to stop what is happening because it is already done. One cannot salvage, one cannot cure – the victim is already dead. Here it is time to leave things in God's hands and affirm His justice and how everything He does is somehow for the best. Because death, destruction – anything that is outside the realm of life – is none of our business. It is God's domain. It is now time not to challenge the Almighty, but to attempt to find comfort in Him.

So Abraham tries to do whatever he can to save Sodom. He begs God, "May the Lord not be angry, but let me speak just once more" (Genesis 18:32), and then once again, and again. He gallantly takes the supreme Master of the universe to court and tells Him that the destruction of Sodom is not just. But once he has done everything within his ability, once Abraham has exercised his full capacity for defense and the affirmation of life, "Abraham returned home" (Genesis 18:33). After discharging his obligation, Abraham returned home with the full confidence that he had done everything within his ability and now it was time to put his trust in God that whatever would happen would be just and fair. Abraham now looked for solace in the one, true, and loving God who desires what is best for the earth's inhabitants.

We find King David reacting the same way when his first son with Bathsheba lay deathly ill. David had fasted, wept, pleaded, and prayed to God on behalf of the child. But the moment the child died, it all changed:

> David noticed that his attendants were whispering among themselves, and he realized the child was dead. "Is the child dead?" he asked. "Yes," they replied, "he is dead." Then David got up from the ground. After he had washed, put on lotions and changed his clothes, he went into the house of the Lord and worshiped. Then he went to his own house, and at his request they served him food, and he ate. His attendants asked him, "Why are you acting this way? While the child was alive, you fasted and wept, but now that the child is dead, you get up and eat!" He answered, "While the child was still alive, I fasted and wept. I thought, 'Who knows? The Lord may be gracious to me and let the child live.' But now that he is dead, why should I go on fasting? Can I bring him back again? I will go to him, but he will not return to me." (II Samuel 12:19–23).

There is a time for protest, for fighting with all our hearts for justice, for kindness, for good, and in the end, when we have done all we can, there is a time for acceptance. *Challenging God and accepting God's will are not in contradiction: they are both critical parts of a vibrant faith.*

## CHAPTER 18

# WHAT THE WORLD NEEDS FROM YOU

---

I love you, Lord, my strength. The Lord is my rock, my fortress and my deliverer; my God is my rock, in whom I take refuge, my shield and the horn of my salvation, my stronghold. I called to the Lord, who is worthy of praise, and I have been saved from my enemies. *(Psalms 18:1–3)*

The Lord is close to the brokenhearted and saves those who are crushed in spirit. *(Psalms 34:18)*

"For I know the plans I have for you," declares the Lord, "plans to prosper you and not to harm you, plans to give you hope and a future." *(Jeremiah 29:11)*

---

So, after all is said and done, how should we respond to suffering? What is the proper response? How do we approach those who have lost children, whose bodies are riddled with cancer, who have experienced financial ruin, and who have babies born without arms or legs?

Is it merely a matter of merely telling them that they should never accept their suffering but should rail against the injustice and thunder against God? Is it about telling them that there is no point to their suffering, that it ought never to have happened, and that all who find justification for their suffering are doing them a further injustice?

How can any of this provide real comfort? How can it comfort people against their pain? Even as you tell them this, they are still suffering. Even as you relate to them that suffering has no redemptive purpose, you're not making it go away. So of what value is everything I've written?

This is exactly what a mother who lost a daughter told me.

More than a decade ago I was delivering a series of lectures on why innocent people suffer that ultimately served to help me develop the core ideas of this book. It was an eight-part lecture series in a private home. Every Monday night a middle-aged woman came to the lecture and sat all the way in back. As soon as it finished she departed, before anyone else. After the eighth and final lecture was delivered, the people slowly left but she remained behind. When the room was empty she approached me and told me her name. "I've come to every part of your series to find comfort. I wanted you to take away my agony. About three years ago my twenty-eight-year-old daughter, a mother of two young children, was on the phone with me one morning when the line went dead. We tried to reach her and finally sent around an ambulance. She had had a brain embolism and died three days later. I have had no consolation and thought you might provide it. But you have left me empty."

I looked at the woman and said, "I am so sorry for the tragedy you've suffered. I apologize for letting you down. But in a way, that was my whole purpose. My point was to say that your daughter was so special that no explanation could take her place. Could you just imagine if you could lose a daughter and then come to some lecture delivered by a rabbi and the pain goes away? How precious then was your daughter, that a mere speech, a collection of words, a rationalization, could supplant the hurt you feel upon her loss?

"No," I continued. "I am right, even if it hurts. Your daughter is more important, was infinitely more precious, than a book, a speech, or any explanation as to why she died. Anything that could be said is just an insult against her memory. I am here not to take away your pain but to validate it. It is justified. It is righteous. It is real. Your daughter should never have died. We should make no peace with it."

And this, essentially, is what Elie Wiesel told one thousand Oxford students when I brought him to lecture at the Oxford Union. After Wiesel gave a masterful and beautiful speech about the Holocaust, an Asian student, tears flowing down his cheeks, stood up to ask, "So why, Professor Wiesel, why did it happen? How could God have allowed it?" The student was choking on his words. Wiesel waited till there was absolute silence. He bowed his head, still waiting, then looked up and said, "I cannot answer your question. I know you are asking it with tremendous feeling and I am deeply attuned to the loving place in your heart whence it came. But I cannot answer it because it is an immoral question. For were I to answer it, were I to offer you a beautiful explanation as to why it happened, then you might sleep easier tonight. The full horror of the Holocaust would be diminished, and you would sleep easier."

We're not supposed to sleep easier while there is suffering and tragedy in the world. We're supposed to provide comfort to the bereaved. We're supposed to enact justice and punish those who cause it. We're supposed to cure illness, combat death, end poverty, fight hunger, and never allow the beachhead of justification for any of these ills.

There is an apocryphal story told how, after the Holocaust, a group of nine great rabbis traveled back to Poland and conducted a trial of God. The charge was the abandonment of European Jewry to Hitler's monsters. Why was God guilty of allowing the

Holocaust? One rabbi served as prosecuting attorney, the other as defense attorney, and seven as judges. Back and forth the deliberations went until a verdict was reached. The rabbis found God to be guilty as charged. And just as soon as they reached their verdict, they went out of their makeshift courtroom to find a tenth Jew to make a minyan (the necessary quorum) and daven Minchah, the afternoon prayer.

**How could great rabbis have found God guilty of such crimes and then prayed to Him? Because both were religious obligations.** The responsibility to affirm life is something that God had commanded them and was no less important than the responsibility to pray thrice daily.

On my television show *Shalom in the Home* I met an extraordinary woman named Carolyn Moore who was widowed of her beloved husband at the age of thirty-six. It was Valentine's Day and they were returning from a romantic dinner when their car crashed. Her husband suffered severe head trauma and died in her lap. She kept the bloody dress under her bed. Six years later a morbid atmosphere pervaded the home. Somber black-and-white photos of her husband hung on the walls. She showed her daughters endless videos of their father, telling them he is lost and there will never be another like him.

I told her, "Your mourning period is up. Just as an explanation for death lends it dignity, excessive mourning does the same. Stop accommodating death. Stop giving it sanction in your home. On the last day of his life Moses gathered around the people of Israel and told them, 'Today I place before you life and death. You must choose life.' We must always choose life. But sometimes, death chooses us. It barges into our lives. Breaks down the door and becomes an unwelcome visitor in our homes. But even when that happens – and we can't always stop it – that still doesn't mean we have to welcome death and treat him as an honored guest. Death is a thief, death is an intruder. Death dare not be granted any quarter in our life. Stop remembering the husband that died and remember instead the husband who lived. Instead of portraying your husband's life as having been cursed, we will make your husband's memory into a blessing.

"From now on, you and your two daughters will do good things in your husband's memory. You will visit the elderly, volunteer in soup kitchens, and go to visit other families who have experienced terrible loss. The idea here is not to dignify death, but to prolong life. So long as you are doing good things in the name of your husband, he still has an impact on the living. And in that way, his life continues. He is still relevant. He is, in part, with you." Carolyn and her daughters removed the haunting black-and-white photos from the walls and replaced them with vibrant color pictures that were all smiles. And they started visiting elderly people in their neighborhood because Chad, their father, had always loved and been so kind to his grandparents and the elderly people he met.

An Orthodox Jewish husband and wife with whom I was acquainted in London lost a daughter in a car accident. The young woman was nineteen. The father stopped going to synagogue. He found he could not pray. I met him and told him I completely understood. "You do?" he asked me. "All the other rabbis were telling me that God had done this for a reason and it was a good reason and I just had to accept it. I should pray and find comfort in God."

"Those other rabbis," I said, "are well-meaning. But they are encouraging you to have a fraudulent relationship with God. Find comfort in God? He took your baby girl from you. And you have every right to be angry. If you don't feel like praying, don't pray. Go to synagogue and sit in righteous indignation. Go to synagogue to confront Him. Just don't run from Him. Don't let Him off the hook. Have an honest relationship with God. For you have more faith than the rabbis. You believe that God controls everything in the world, and that's why you're so angry at Him.

"But remember, just as you are rightly angry for the bad, fairness dictates that you have to give credit for the good. You have three other healthy children. You have a wife who loves you and you are finding comfort in each other. And no, these things will never compensate for, or replace, the loss you've suffered. But they do show that there are still great blessings in your life. Thank God for the good He gives you and rail against the injustice He has inflicted on you. Make it a real relationship, not just with God but with your daughter as well. Do good things in her name. Help those who are experiencing similar pain. Show your daughter that her memory continues to influence you and that she is forever relevant in your life.

"And over time, you will see that your desire to keep God's rituals will return. The *tefillin* that you today shun will become a comfort to you, as you bind yourself in God's grace. The *tallit*, prayer shawl, you refuse to don will become a sacred blanket in which you find comfort and warmth. Don't rush it. But it will happen. And when it does, your relationship with God will still be broken and incomplete, as will you. But, as the Kotzker Rebbe said, there is nothing more whole than a shattered heart."

This father, who is a psychiatrist, started giving free counsel to ten patients a week who could not afford it, all in his daughter's name, to alleviate their suffering. And with that he dignified not her death but her life. His religious feelings remain tenuous. But in an effort to inspire his other children to continue Jewish tradition, he has begun reconnecting with his faith.

# CHAPTER 19

# THE LESSON OF JOB

And here is where we can end off with the most famous biblical story of all, Job, and draw the proper lessons. We quoted from the book of Job before, showing he had lost everything although he was righteous. He rails and thunders against God. He knows he doesn't deserve his suffering. His friends come and castigate him for fighting back. How dare he question God? It is his sin that has caused him to suffer so. But Job is adamant. He knows he is righteous. He knows he has done nothing wrong. He refuses to give in, and just then, everything changes. God Himself suddenly appears to Job out of the whirlwind. God's speech to Job is so moving and so earthshattering that it is worth quoting in full:

> Then the Lord spoke to Job out of the storm. He said: "Who is this that obscures my plans with words without knowledge? Brace yourself like a man; I will question you, and you shall answer me. Where were you when I laid the earth's foundation? Tell me, if you understand. Who marked off its dimensions? Surely you know! Who stretched a measuring line across it? On what were its footings set, or who laid its cornerstone – while the morning stars sang together and all the angels shouted for joy? Who shut up the sea behind doors when it burst forth from the womb, when I made the clouds its garment and wrapped it in thick darkness, when I fixed limits for it and set its doors and bars in place, when

I said, 'This far you may come and no farther; here is where your proud waves halt'? Have you ever given orders to the morning, or shown the dawn its place, that it might take the earth by the edges and shake the wicked out of it? The earth takes shape like clay under a seal; its features stand out like those of a garment. The wicked are denied their light, and their upraised arm is broken. Have you journeyed to the springs of the sea or walked in the recesses of the deep? Have the gates of death been shown to you? Have you seen the gates of the deepest darkness? Have you comprehended the vast expanses of the earth? Tell me, if you know all this. What is the way to the abode of light? And where does darkness reside? Can you take them to their places? Do you know the paths to their dwellings? Surely you know, for you were already born! You have lived so many years! Have you entered the storehouses of the snow or seen the storehouses of the hail, which I reserve for times of trouble, for days of war and battle? What is the way to the place where the lightning is dispersed, or the place where the east winds are scattered over the earth? Who cuts a channel for the torrents of rain, and a path for the thunderstorm, to water a land where no one lives, an uninhabited desert, to satisfy a desolate wasteland and make it sprout with grass? Does the rain have a father? Who fathers the drops of dew? From whose womb comes the ice? Who gives birth to the frost from the heavens when the waters become hard as stone, when the surface of the deep is frozen? Can you bind the chains of the Pleiades? Can you loosen Orion's belt? Can you bring forth the constellations in their seasons or lead out the Bear with its cubs? Do you know the laws of the heavens? Can you set up God's dominion over the earth? Can you raise your voice to the clouds and cover yourself with a flood of water? Do you send the lightning bolts on their way? Do they report to you, 'Here we are'? Who gives the ibis wisdom or gives the rooster understanding? Who has the wisdom to count the clouds? Who can tip over the water jars of the heavens when the dust becomes hard and the clods of earth stick together? Do you hunt the prey for the lioness and satisfy the hunger of the lions when they crouch in their dens or lie in wait in a thicket? Who provides food for the raven when its young cry out to God and wander about for lack of food?" (Job 38)

God is saying to Job, *How dare you question Me? I am so infinitely large that you, a mere mortal, could never understand Me or the vast universe into which you are immersed. So how dare you question? Could you ever possibly fathom the vast magnitude of My responsibilities, how I keep all the planets suspended in their orbits, and fill the infinite expanse of space. Who are you that you question Me? How could you ever even attempt to understand My ways or question them? Take your suffering like a man. Perhaps it is good for you. How do you know it is not? Do you know the secrets of the universe? Do you know the mysteries of the cosmos? Do you provide food for all the earth's animals? Did you create life and do you know how to sustain it?*

"Do you know when the mountain goats give birth? Do you watch when the doe bears her fawn? Do you count the months till they bear? Do you know the time they give birth? They crouch down and bring forth their young; their labor pains are ended. Their young thrive and grow strong in the wilds; they leave and do not return. Who let the wild donkey go free? Who untied its ropes? I gave it the wasteland as its home, the salt flats as its habitat. It laughs at the commotion in the town; it does not hear a driver's shout. It ranges the hills for its pasture and searches for any green thing. Will the wild ox consent to serve you? Will it stay by your manger at night? Can you hold it to the furrow with a harness? Will it till the valleys behind you? Will you rely on it for its great strength? Will you leave your heavy work to it? Can you trust it to haul in your grain and bring it to your threshing floor? The wings of the ostrich flap joyfully, though they cannot compare with the wings and feathers of the stork. She lays her eggs on the ground and lets them warm in the sand, unmindful that a foot may crush them, that some wild animal may trample them. She treats her young harshly, as if they were not hers; she cares not that her labor was in vain, for God did not endow her with wisdom or give her a share of good sense. Yet when she spreads her feathers to run, she laughs at horse and rider. Do you give the horse its strength or clothe its neck with a flowing mane? Do you make it leap like a locust, striking terror with its proud snorting? It paws fiercely, rejoicing in its strength, and charges into the fray. It laughs at fear, afraid of nothing; it does not shy away from the sword. The quiver rattles against its side, along with the flashing spear and lance. In frenzied excitement it eats up the ground; it cannot stand still when the trumpet sounds. At the blast of the trumpet it snorts, 'Aha!' It catches the scent of battle from afar, the shout of commanders and the battle cry. Does the hawk take flight by your wisdom and spread its wings toward the south? Does the eagle soar at your command and build its nest on high? It dwells on a cliff and stays there at night; a rocky crag is its stronghold. From there it looks for food; its eyes detect it from afar. Its young ones feast on blood, and where the slain are, there it is." The Lord said to Job: "Will the one who contends with the Almighty correct him? Let him who accuses God answer him!" (Job 39:1–40:2)

And with this incredibly moving speech, it seems as though the matter has now been decided. God is saying to Job, *You have no right to question Me. You have no right to challenge Me. I feed and sustain all the earth's creatures. I provide sustenance to all life and care for all existence. There are mysteries that are utterly beyond your comprehension in a universe so vast your puny human mind could scarcely apprehend even its smallest details. Suffering happens for a purpose and that's that. And if you want to challenge Me on suffering, Job, if you're such a know-it-all, then you can't challenge Me with half measures. You need to run the world and order the universe. If you're so much better at this than Me, then be a man and take over.*

And this seems to be exactly what other religious figures have told me when I have advocated, as I have throughout this book, that we must challenge God in the face of suffering. We have no right to challenge God. It is blasphemous and arrogant. We must believe in His goodness and accept our licks as the loving discipline that comes from on high. God always has a plan.

Indeed, Job himself, now moved and utterly broken by God's personal intervention, gives in completely.

In a moving confession, he says: "I am unworthy – how can I reply to you? I put my hand over my mouth. I spoke once, but I have no answer – twice, but I will say no more" (Job 40:4–5).

Job, it seems, has lost completely. He's done. Outwitted. By God Himself. God has triumphed completely over him. He has broken a once defiant Job, who is now helpless and compliant. Beaten completely into submission, a once rebellious man is now utterly silent.

But God is not finished with him. He castigates him further:

Then the Lord spoke to Job out of the storm: "Brace yourself like a man; I will question you, and you shall answer me.

Would you discredit my justice? Would you condemn me to justify yourself? Do you have an arm like God's, and can your voice thunder like his? Then adorn yourself with glory and splendor, and clothe yourself in honor and majesty. Unleash the fury of your wrath, look at all who are proud and bring them low, look at all who are proud and humble them, crush the wicked where they stand. Bury them all in the dust together; shroud their faces in the grave. Then I myself will admit to you that your own right hand can save you." (Job 40:6–14)

More defeated than ever, Job, like a crawling worm, begs for forgiveness:

Then Job replied to the Lord: "I know that you can do all things; no purpose of yours can be thwarted. You asked, 'Who is this that obscures my plans without knowledge?' Surely I spoke of things I did not understand, things too wonderful for me to know. You said, 'Listen now, and I will speak; I will question you, and you shall answer me.' My ears had heard of you but now my eyes have seen you. Therefore I despise myself and repent in dust and ashes." (Job 42:1–6)

And with that the story should end. Job should suffer. He is guilty, either because he is indeed sinful, although he cannot identify how so, or he is guilty of monumental human ignorance. As a limited mortal human, he cannot peer behind the divine veil. God has been vindicated, man has been implicated. God is innocent and man is guilty. Religion has triumphed. Faith has prevailed. Job can now return to his wretched little human existence, suffused with suffering and tragedy, and take his licks like a good, pious, religious mortal. He was once the fed-up man of faith, the rebellious man of religion, unwilling to accept undeserved suffering, prepared to thunder and rail against the heavens in demanding justice. Now, he is the suffering man of the spirit, cracked and smashed, ruined and destroyed. He dared challenge the heavens and he has fallen like a meteor back down to earth.

And the end of this story should prove the end of my book as well. My theory has been defeated. My advocacy for religious rebelliousness has been repudiated. God confronted Job and God won. The battle between Deity and human is over, with the Divine having carried the day. I should delete this book from my computer hard drive, where it was written, and never allow it to see the light of day.

And yet, you are still reading it. And why? *Because Job's story does not end there.* Remarkably, the end of the story, the very last chapter of Job, reads thus:

> After the Lord had said these things to Job, he said to Eliphaz the Temanite, "I am angry with you and your two friends, because you have not spoken the truth about me, as my servant Job has. So now take seven bulls and seven rams and go to my servant Job and sacrifice a burnt offering for yourselves. My servant Job will pray for you, and I will accept his prayer and not deal with you according to your folly. You have not spoken the truth about me, as my servant Job has." So Eliphaz the Temanite, Bildad the Shuhite and Zophar the Naamathite did what the Lord told them; and the Lord accepted Job's prayer. After Job had prayed for his friends, the Lord restored his fortunes and gave him twice as much as he had before. All his brothers and sisters and everyone who had known him before came and ate with him in his house. They comforted and consoled him over all the trouble the Lord had brought on him, and each one gave him

a piece of silver and a gold ring. The Lord blessed the latter part of Job's life more than the former part. He had fourteen thousand sheep, six thousand camels, a thousand yoke of oxen and a thousand donkeys. And he also had seven sons and three daughters. The first daughter he named Jemimah, the second Keziah and the third Keren-Happuch. Nowhere in all the land were there found women as beautiful as Job's daughters, and their father granted them an inheritance along with their brothers. After this, Job lived a hundred and forty years; he saw his children and their children to the fourth generation. And so Job died, an old man and full of years. (Job 42:7-17)

The story ends with God castigating Job's so-called friends for telling him that he was sinful and had no right to challenge God. Those who find fault in others, who tell them they suffer for their sins, are themselves sinful. God even tells them that Job alone is righteous and must even pray for them. Job alone has a real relationship with God because he alone is prepared to go beyond the fraudulence and actually challenge God when injustice seems to prevail. God likes the sparky Job. He invites his challenge. Sure, he pushes back. He rebukes Job. As we said before and as the Torah in Deuteronomy 29:29 makes clear, "The secret things belong to the Lord our God, but the things revealed belong to us and to our children forever."

God will always protect His domain. He is God. He must run the universe. But none of that has anything to do with us. Our job as humans is to protect life, promote life, and affirm life. Our role is to challenge God and demand that innocent people live long, happy, healthy lives without suffering or loss. And when God allows the righteous to suffer, our job is to question God and demand that the pain end and that death be banished.

And even when God speaks to us from the whirlwind, we may give in for but a moment, but it is really God Who gives in completely. For in the end – and this is key – *God did exactly what Job had demanded.* God took away the suffering. He ended his pain not by providing an explanation for Job's loss but by making good the loss. He restored Job's property and wealth, which he had earned through righteousness. Most importantly, he gave Job ten beautiful children. Not that they could ever replace those lost, but he restored children to him nonetheless. (There is even a rabbinic tradition, cited by Nahmanides, that Job's original children were restored to him.[1]) It is Job's victory that is complete. God acquiesces completely. It is God Who gives in.

And so our book is complete. *The real answer to suffering is to do as Job. Assert your righteousness, hold God accountable, challenge fate, and demand that suffering finally end.* Comfort the bereaved, give charity to the poor. Feed the hungry, clothe the naked. Rail against injustice. Stand up for those bent by suffering. Mend the hearts of those racked with pain. And, by standing in God's stead and doing what He should be doing, though He remain silent, shame God into action. Show Him that we do all this because He himself commanded it. He himself said that suffering must be defeated and that life must be prolonged. He said that life is infinitely precious and must be saved at all costs. And it is time, high time, that, as He did with Job, he finally keep His promise, and grant life, liberty, and happiness to all His earthly children.

May it soon be so.

---

1   The wording of the text is very particular when describing the children that God gave Job afterward. In one interpretation, when the verse states in the last chapter of Job, "And he also had seven sons and three daughters," it is not informing us that he had ten new children, but that in actuality his children had never died. Job had been misinformed the entire time about his progeny's fate.

# OTHER BOOKS BY SHMULEY BOTEACH

*A Modern Guide to Judaism* (2012)

*The Portable Shmuley: Selected Writing by Rabbi Shmuley Boteach* (2012)

*Kosher Jesus* (Gefen Publishing House, 2012)

*10 Conversations You Need to Have with Yourself: A Powerful Plan for Spiritual Growth and Self-Improvement* (2011)

*Honoring the Child Spirit: Inspiration and Learning from Our Children* (2011)

*Renewal: A Guide to the Values-Filled Life* (2010)

*The Blessings of Enough: Rejecting Material Greed, Embracing Spiritual Hunger* (2010)

*The Michael Jackson Tapes: A Tragic Icon Reveals His Soul in Intimate Conversation* (2009)

*The Broken American Male: And How to Fix Him* (2008)

*The Kosher Sutra: Eight Sacred Secrets for Reigniting Desire and Restoring Passion for Life* (2009)

*Shalom in the Home: Smart Advice for a Peaceful Life* (2007)

*Parenting with Fire: Lighting Up the Family with Passion and Inspiration* (2006)

*10 Conversations You Need to Have with Your Children* (2006)

*An Intelligent Person's Guide to Judaism* (2006)

*Hating Women: America's Hostile Campaign against the Fairer Sex* (2005)

*Face Your Fear: Living with Courage in an Age of Caution* (2004)

*The Private Adam: Becoming a Hero in a Selfish Age* (2003)

*Judaism for Everyone: Renewing Your Life through the Vibrant Lessons of the Jewish Faith* (2002)

*Kosher Adultery: Seduce and Sin with your Spouse* (2002)

*Why Can't I Fall in Love: A 12-Step Program* (2001)

*The Psychic and the Rabbi: A Remarkable Correspondence* (co-authored with Uri Geller, 2001)

*True Confessions* (co-authored with Uri Geller, 2000)

*Dating Secrets of the Ten Commandments* (2000)

*Kosher Emotions: Understand Your Emotions and Master Your Life* (2000)

*Kosher Sex: A Recipe for Passion and Intimacy* (1999)

*The Jewish Guide to Adultery: How to Turn Your Marriage into an Illicit Affair* (1995)

*Moses of Oxford: A Jewish Vision of a University and Its Life*, volumes 1 and 2 (with introductions by Norman Stone and Danah Zohar, 1994)

*Wrestling with the Divine: A Jewish Response to Suffering* (1994)

*The Wolf Shall Lie with the Lamb: The Messiah in Hasidic Thought* (1993)

*Wisdom, Understanding, and Knowledge: Basic Concepts of Hasidic Thought* (1992)

*Dreams* (1991)